IGNITING

JOY

IN 40 DAYS

IGNITING JOY IN 40 DAYS

STEVE BACKLUND

WITH DR. PIETER LAGAAY

Igniting Joy in 40 Days
Copyright 2023 by Steve Backlund, Igniting Hope Ministries
www.ignitinghope.com

ISBN: 978-1-7363601-6-3

Cover design credit: Zoltan Hercik
Interior layout and formatting: Eugene Rijn Saratorio

Many thanks to the following who helped with editing this book: Shelter Musavengana, Ash Anderson and Angela Parker

If you enjoy this book and want more, go to ignitinghope.com to find:

- Blogs and podcasts
- Books and resources
- Information on the Backlunds' speaking itinerary
- The contact form for Steve or Wendy about speaking to your group
- Many free resources to inspire your life
- Online events to ignite your hope

TABLE OF CONTENTS

ABOUT THE AUTHORS

Steve Backlund is an encourager, leader developer, joy activist, and a revivalist teacher. He has a unique gift to release hope and joy in his speaking, writings, and in his leadership. Steve and his wife Wendy were senior pastors for seventeen years and now reside in Redding, CA. He is the Associate Director of the Bethel Leaders Network, and with his wife Wendy founded Igniting Hope Ministries and the Igniting Hope Academy. The Backlunds have three children and seven grand-children.

"Steve Backlund is known for his wisdom and practical insights on how to do life. The students in our ministry school, Bethel School of Supernatural Ministry, love him because he always leaves them encouraged and refreshed in their vision. He has an unusual gift to take the mundane and make it exciting and to take the familiar and make it new."

Bill Johnson, Bethel Church, Redding, CA
Author of *When Heaven Invades Earth*

Pieter Lagaay was born in Berkeley, CA, and got his bachelor's degree in Molecular, Cellular, and Developmental Biology from the University of California, Santa Cruz. Thereafter, Pieter obtained a Doctorate in Podiatric Medicine from Temple University and completed a surgical foot and ankle residency with Kaiser Permanente. Pieter furthered his postdoctoral training with an AO orthopedic lower extremity trauma fellowship at the Carl Gustav Carus University in Dresden, Germany, and a pediatric orthopedic clubfoot fellowship at the University of Iowa. As an attending, Pieter served as a residency research director, pediatric surgery instructor, trauma surgery instructor, and peer review editor for the Journal of Foot and Ankle Surgery. After ten years of practicing medicine, Pieter attended law school at night while practicing medicine during the day. He obtained his Juris Doctorate from John F. Kennedy University Law School.

In 2015, before being saved, when his marriage was falling apart due to his infidelity, Pieter had a radical encounter with God through an open vision. While on his knees, feeling hopeless about his marriage and the seemingly unbreakable grip of his addiction to porn and lust, all he could utter was, "I can't fix this." This was all it took for Jesus to meet Pieter where he was at.

Pieter's salvation journey and the road to freedom from sexual immorality and restoration of his marriage prompted him to publish his first book, "Silently Broken, Loudly Restored." This book gives hope that nothing is beyond the restorative power of Jesus Christ.

In 2020 Pieter and his wife Melinda moved to Redding, CA, to attend ministry school at the Bethel School of Supernatural Ministry. While in school, they co-founded Arise and Shine Ministries, which focuses on inner healing and deliverance. The Lagaays have a heart to see what Jesus did in their lives and marriage for other people. Pieter and Melinda have three beautiful children and are now dreaming together about how God will use them for His glory in the years to come.

INTRODUCTION

"Joy is one-third of the Kingdom."

When I first heard someone say this, I said to myself, "I don't think so." But as I have grown in the Lord, I now fully believe it. To pursue joy (not be passive about it), we must overcome negative mindsets limiting our lives (victimhood, unworthiness, pessimism, impulsiveness, fear, offense, disappointment, etc.). I imagine it like a person heading up to the top of the mountain of joy carrying a backpack. In that backpack are beliefs, attitudes, and habits that must be removed the higher he/she goes. At one point or another, we are this person. We can't take offense up there. We can't take the critical spirit up there. We can't take perfectionism up there. We can't take shame and unworthiness up there. As we shed these things, we begin to experience consistent joy. I remember saying to the Lord, "You tricked me. I just wanted to be happy and You made me grow by urging me to prioritize joy as one-third of the kingdom."

Ha ha, God may "trick you" too as you read this book. I believe its content will super-charge you with grace to upgrade your beliefs about God, the people in your life, your future, your current circumstances, and how you see yourself.

We have strategically formatted the book into eight five-day sections. Every fifth day is a time to reflect on the content of the previous four days; plus, we include Dr. Pieter Lagaay's Advanced Research on Joy on that day as well. Dr. Lagaay's scientific insights will convince you even more of the value of joy.

Finally, for those of you who want an even deeper connection with the truths of this book, you can go to www.ignitinghopeacademy.com and receive a short podcast for each devotional in the book (through the mini-course "40 Days of Joy").

I bless you as you ignite your joy in the next forty days.

Steve Backlund

DAY 1
Joy Bible Verses: Part One

"Do not sorrow, for the joy of the Lord is your strength" (Nehemiah 8:10) – We don't need strength at the end of the battle; we need strength in the middle of the battle. For most people reading this right now, today is not a good day to walk in radical joy. I have rarely found a time in my life when it is convenient to walk in great joy. There always seems to be a reason to delay it, but I cannot because it is my strength. I believe that our spiritual load-bearing capacity is in direct proportion to the level of joy in our lives.

"In His presence is fullness of joy" (Psalm 16:11) – "We may not be outrageously joyful every time we are in His presence, but if we are never joyful in His presence, then we may not be in His presence as we much as we think we are." I share this phrase frequently when I speak on joy. I do so to help us expand our view of what might happen when we go deeper into God's presence. Many expect tears, but not as many expect joy and laughter. We have many worship bands that help us experience His presence in incredible ways. We are thankful for them. Equally important are those who help God's people experience joy in His presence through their ministry and lives.

"Serve the Lord with gladness" (Psalm 100:1) – We are told to "serve the Lord with gladness." Regular gladness is one of the signs that we have passed the tests at the level that we are at. If we are consistently not glad in the place we are at, then it will be very difficult for us to succeed at a higher place. "If you have run with the footmen, and they

1

have wearied you, Then how can you contend with horses?" (Jeremiah 12:5). Faithfulness is not just showing up, but it is how we think when we show up. We must show up full of faith (believing we are significant and influential, and what we are doing is important). Again, regular gladness is a sign we are ready for promotion and increase.

"Restore to me the joy of Your salvation" (Psalm 51:12) – I do not want to get as low as David (committing adultery and murder) to pray this powerful prayer. To restore means to return (someone or something) to a former condition, place, or position. David recognized the value of joy, and was intentional in seeing it return. He specifically asks for the "joy of Your salvation" to be returned. What is interesting to me about this is that his "salvation" in the Old Testament is much less valuable than our salvation in the New Testament. We have something greater than David to protect and, if needed, to be restored.

Activation

Read these important truths out loud:

- We don't need strength at the end of the battle; we need strength in the middle of the battle.
- Our spiritual load-bearing capacity is in direct proportion to the level of joy in our lives.
- In His presence is fullness of joy.
- Regular gladness is one of the signs that we have passed the tests at the level that we are at.
- Faithfulness is not just showing up, but it is how we think when we show up.
- David recognized the value of joy, and was intentional in seeing it return.

DAY 2
Joy Bible Verses: Part Two

"Now may the God of hope fill you with all joy and peace in believing, that you may abound in hope by the power of the Holy Spirit" (Romans 15:13) – The key words in this verse are "in believing". The moment we believe truth is the moment we get filled with God's hope. Increasing hope is evidence we are renewing our minds with truth instead of lies. Decreasing hope is evidence we are renewing our minds with lies instead of truth. As we get filled by the God of hope, all joy and peace increase as well. Jesus said, "The truth will make you free" (John 8:32). We first get free in our emotions (hope, joy, and peace) and then in our circumstances. Believing lies causes us to be limited first in our emotions (hopelessness, a lack of joy, anxiety, etc.) and then in our circumstances. Joy and gladness primarily result from having good beliefs.

"But the fruit of the Spirit is love, joy, peace . . ." (Galatians 5:22) – In nature, good fruit comes from healthy trees. The trees do not strive to produce it, but it comes naturally. In the same way, if we are healthy in our spirit and soul, we will produce naturally good "fruit of the Spirit" (and joy is the second one listed). If we are regularly not experiencing joy, the first thing to evaluate is our connection to the Lord. Are we disconnected (or poorly connected) from His love, grace, and His word?

"God has anointed You (Jesus) with the oil of gladness more than Your companions" (Hebrews 1:9) – Jesus created a culture of gladness around him. Great leaders and great parents create a culture of gladness around them. To do this, we must let go of a lot of things that prevent gladness: perfectionism, control, critical attitudes, victim mindset, unworthiness, canceling people, and more.

"Behold, I bring you good tidings of great joy which will be to all people" (Luke 2:10) – I have bookshelves full of different books regarding my faith in Christ. The diversity of topics is astounding. There are books on prayer, love, family, church government, evangelism, prophecy, spiritual gifts, obedience, worship, and many others. I often say I find it very noteworthy that of all the topics heaven could have had the angel speak of to the shepherds concerning the purpose of Jesus, "great joy" was the one chosen. Every time I meditate on this, I am struck by how REALLY important joy is and how I cannot afford to be passive about it.

Activation

Read these important truths out loud:

- Increasing hope is evidence we are renewing our minds with truth instead of lies.
- The truth will make you free.
- Great leaders and great parents create a culture of gladness around them.
- "Great joy" was the focus of the angel's announcement to the shepherds about baby Jesus.

DAY 3
Joy Bible Verses: Part Three

"My brethren, count it all joy when you fall into various trials, knowing that the testing of your faith produces perseverance. But let perseverance have its perfect work, that you may be perfect and complete, lacking nothing (James 1:2-4) – Here are three of my favorite quotes: 1) What is happening in me is more important than what is happening through me, 2) My response to something is almost always more important than the something, and 3) My current challenges and frustrations are my training ground for the greater influence I'll have in the future. James tells us we are to "count it all joy" when we face challenging circumstances because we "know" something positive will result from such trials. Just as we strengthen the muscles in our bodies by pushing against resistance, in the same way, we get to build strong character and belief muscles by pushing against challenging circumstances ("various trials") with God's promises.

"Rejoice in the Lord always. Again I will say, rejoice!" (Philippians 4:4) – We have already discussed how joy is a fruit of a good connection with God (Galatians 5:22) and evidence we are believing truth instead of lies (Romans 15:13). A lack of joy is like the Check Engine Light on a car. It shows something is wrong which needs to be fixed. We don't ignore that light when it starts flashing and so it should be when we constantly lack joy in our lives – we need to do something. It is important to know there will be times when we will need to tell our soul (mind, will, and emotions) to rejoice (feel joyful and be delighted). It is what the Psalmist did. "Why are you cast down, O my soul? And why are you

5

disquieted within me? Hope in God, for I shall yet praise Him" (Psalm 42:5). Rejoicing in the Lord is a decision to magnify the Lord instead of magnifying the problem (Psalm 34:3). It is an assertive, passionate step to believe in the goodness and promises of God. It is necessary to walk in victory.

"For the kingdom of God is not eating and drinking, but righteousness and peace and joy in the Holy Spirit" (Romans 14:17) – "Joy is one-third of the Kingdom." When I first heard someone say this, I said to myself, "I don't think so." But as I have grown in the Lord, I now fully believe it. To pursue joy (not be passive about it), we must overcome negative mindsets limiting our lives (victimhood, unworthiness, pessimism, impulsiveness, fear, offense, disappointment, etc.). I imagine it like a person heading up to the top of the mountain of joy carrying a backpack. In that backpack are attitudes and habits that must be removed the higher he/she goes. At one point or another, we are this person. We can't take offense up there. We can't take the critical spirit up there. We can't take perfectionism up there. We can't take shame and unworthiness up there. As we shed these things, we begin to experience consistent joy. I remember saying to the Lord, "You tricked me. I just wanted to be happy and You made me grow by urging me to prioritize joy as one-third of the kingdom."

"He who would love life and see good days, let him refrain his tongue from evil, and his lips from speaking deceit" (1 Peter 3:10) – There is a difference between loving God and loving and enjoying life. The Amplified version actually says, "He who would enjoy life . . ." I have found it rarely convenient to really enjoy (take delight and pleasure in) life. I am either in a hurry to get somewhere or have a romantic view of the future that there will be a much more ideal time to love and enjoy life. I find it fascinating that this verse is in the Bible. It is an invitation to activate the abundant life Jesus promised (John 10:10). And, it is significant that this type of living is directly connected to what comes out of our mouths ("let him refrain his tongue from evil, and his lips from speaking deceit"). Those who take control of their words and defeat the tendency of speaking lies about their identity in Christ, their circumstances, and their future, will dramatically increase the likelihood of loving life and seeing good days.

Activation

Read these important truths out loud:

- What is happening in me is more important than what is happening through me.
- My response to something is almost always more important than the something.
- My current challenges and frustrations are my training ground for the greater influence I'll have in the future.
- There will be times when we will need to tell our soul (mind, will, and emotions) to rejoice (feel joyful and delighted).
- Joy is one-third of the kingdom.
- We are empowered to not only love God but to love life also.
- Our joy level will be greatly impacted by how we speak.

DAY 4
Joy Bible Verses: Part Four

"Delight yourself also in the Lord, and He shall give you the desires of your heart" (Psalm 37:4) – The context of this verse is this: the delighter is delighting with unfulfilled desires (with disappointments, outcomes he wants to happen which have not happened yet, etc.). Delighting is a key to seeing God-inspired desires fulfilled. Delighters are hope-filled people. They believe God has many avenues to fulfill their dreams and life purpose. On the contrary, faith people without hope tend to "put all their eggs in one basket" – believing their happiness and destiny are dependent on a specific happening. Faith indeed is specific, while hope is more general. Faith says, "This is going to happen," while Hope says, "I don't know what is going to happen, but good things are coming." Faith people without hope have a very difficult time overcoming disappointment because of a belief system that says, "I can only delight when certain outcomes happen." Hope people say, "Even if that does not happen, I will thrive in life, and I will thrive while I am waiting for it to happen." Faith people with hope are delighters. The delighter's mantra is, "Lord, I cannot wait to see what you are going to do in this situation." Delighting in the Lord is an important aspect of joy.

"A merry heart does good, like medicine" (Proverbs 17 21) – "Doctor God" said, "Steve, I have a prescription for you. Laugh heartily three times a day. It will help you." Science has caught up with the Bible again by proving the health benefits of laughter. If you do an online search for laughter and health, you will find research studies that will inspire more intentional laughter. In each of our eight devotional sections, we have devoted the fifth day to focus on insight and information on the health benefits of laughter and cheerfulness.

"Rejoicing in hope" (Romans 12:12) – In Romans 12, Paul releases some rapid-fire admonitions in verses 9-21 that include "rejoicing in hope". Here are three definitions of hope to rejoice in. 1) Hope is the belief that the future will be better than the present, and I/we have the power to help make it so. 2) Hope is the confident, joyful expectation that good is coming. 3) Hope is an overall optimistic attitude about the future based on the goodness and promises of God. "Let us hold fast the confession of *our* hope without wavering, for He who promised *is* faithful" (Hebrews 10:23). I am not a proponent of positive thinking but of biblical optimism. As we rejoice in hope, our optimism will be an incredibly positive, catalytic force for ourselves and those around us.

"He who sits in the heavens laughs" (Psalms 2:4) – The context of this passage is about God laughing at what His enemies are saying and planning. When I read Psalm 2:4, I had an idea. I am a spiritual experimenter, and I have done many things I have never heard any other person do. So, as I thought about this verse, I decided to experiment by laughing at the lies of the devil. The devil is my enemy, and he is the father of all lies (John 8:44). Lies are the only real weapon that he has, and when we come into agreement with his lies, we empower them. Lies sound very real in the darkness of our thinking, but they are laughable when we bring them into the light of language and words. For instance, I used to believe that I was not saved when I did not feel saved. However, when I spoke the lie out loud, "My salvation is dependent upon my feelings," I realized this was just stupid (and laughable). As we consider why laughing at lies is powerful, I want to say one more thing: to laugh we have to let go of something. When we are able to laugh at the lies creating our negative strongholds, we start to pull down those strongholds and demolish the arguments that are trying to exalt themselves above the knowledge of God in our lives (2 Corinthians 10:4-5).

Activation

Read these important truths out loud:

- Delighters believe God has many avenues to fulfill their dreams and life purpose.
- Science has caught up with the Bible again by proving the health benefits of laughter.
- Laughter is a powerful spiritual weapon that disempowers the lies creating our negative strongholds.
- Hope is the confident, joyful expectation that good is coming.
- Hope is an overall optimistic attitude about the future based on the goodness and promises of God

DAY 5
Reflection, Activation, and Advanced Research on Joy

Joy is the child-like wonder and excitement of working with God instead of working for God.

Steve Backlund

Here are some opening reflection questions. (These become even more powerful if you have someone to discuss your answers with).

1. Which Bible verse from this week spoke to you the most and why?
2. What is the one sentence you read in these past four days which seems like a "now" word for you in this season?
3. Who can you invite to participate with you in this 40 Days of Joy journey?

Activation

Ideas for getting this joy message deeper into you:

1. Start a joy group discussing this devotional's content.
2. Listen to the podcasts from a part of the 40 Days Joy course.. They are short and can be found on ignitinghopeacademy.com.
3. Read Steve's book, *Possessing Joy*, to enhance your experience with this devotional.

4. Celebrate progress, not perfection, in your journey of walking in higher levels of joy.

Advanced Research on Joy by Dr. Pieter Lagaay
Joy Increases Our Ability to Learn

In 1999 a study in the journal, *Biological Psychiatry*, published that joy produced an increase in dopamine in our brains. This increase in dopamine release also demonstrated an increased ability to learn. Although the relationship between the amount of dopamine and the ability to learn does have a sweet spot, this study does demonstrate the biochemical effect joy has on our brain to learn. In 2005 a study in the Journal, *Cognition and Emotion*, revealed that joy was associated with a greater ability to see the big picture (seeing the forest before the trees) vs. just seeing the small task at hand (seeing the trees before the forest). Additionally, joy was correlated with stronger problem-solving.

Jesus "was anointed with the oil of gladness above all his companions" (Hebrews 1:9). He created a culture of gladness around Him which enhanced the learning (discipleship) and problem-solving of His disciples. We would be wise as parents, teachers, pastors, bosses, and leaders to value joy, cheerfulness, and laughter as an important part of helping others become all they were meant to be.

We can all grow in our own joy and in our ability to create a culture of gladness around us. Abraham Lincoln said, "People are just as happy as they make up their minds to be." He understood that joy is a mindset that we determine. The realization that Abraham Lincoln had was biochemically validated 200 years later in a 2000 study titled Cultivating Positive Emotions. This publication noted that joy is arguably the single most important factor for enhancing life satisfaction and success, and, thus, creating an incredible atmosphere of personal growth for ourselves and others.

Activation

1. Set a reminder for yourself to increase the culture of gladness in key environments you are a part of.
2. Partner with someone in your home, job, classroom, or organization to develop a strategy to increase the culture of gladness.
3. Share a joke at the beginning of meetings to get people to laugh.
4. When facing a challenging situation that needs a solution, experiment with watching funny animal videos or participating in some other fun and funny activity. Then note whether there is an increase of wisdom and ideas to solve the challenge.

DAY 6
Delight Yourself in the Lord

"Delight yourself also in the Lord, and He will give you the desires of your heart"

(Psalm 37:4).

This wonderful Old Testament promise reinforces 3 John 2: "Beloved, I pray that you may prosper in all things and be in health, just as your soul prospers."

Delighting in the Lord and soul prosperity are two ingredients of overcoming, joy-filled, influential followers of Jesus. They are evidence of winning the inner victories necessary to experience the outer victory described in these two verses (prosperity in all things, being in health, and experiencing the desires of your heart).

When I speak of soul prosperity, let me remind you of two key phrases:

- My response to something is almost always more important than the "something".
- What is happening in me is more important than what is happening through me.

Both of these phrases inspire me to win inner battles by giving me a vision of the long-term benefits of doing so. Soul prosperity dramatically increases the likelihood of seeing the promises of God in our lives. It is the catalytic component that makes our faith declarations unstoppable.

"Delight yourself also in the Lord, and He will give you the desires of your heart." To delight means to "take pleasure in." Pleasure is a feeling of happy satisfaction and enjoyment. We could rephrase the verse, "Enjoy yourself in the Lord." To do so is an incredible sign of faith and Christian maturity.

Just as we need to let go of something to laugh, the same is true for delighting and enjoying ourselves in the Lord. We cannot do this unless we let go of perfectionism, works of the law living, unworthiness, excessive introspection, disappointment, and worry.

Intentional delighting in the Lord is a way to overcome the spirit of heaviness that is referred to in Isaiah 61. "The Spirit of the Lord God . . .has anointed me . . .to give . . .the garment of praise for the spirit of heaviness" (Isaiah 61:1-3). Heaviness is a feeling that everything seems harder than it really is. A spirit of heaviness makes circumstances feel worse than they really are. Often, there is no real thought or logic behind it, but just a feeling and sense that there is no solution, and that things will only get worse.

Delight has the word "light" in it. I know there have been many times I have had to just lighten up. Childlikeness is a key to delighting and lightening up. Jesus states the importance of this.

"Assuredly, I say to you, unless you are converted and become as little children, you will by no means enter the kingdom of heaven" (Matthew 18:3). There are many aspects of kingdom life that cannot be entered into unless we become childlike, and delighting is one of its greatest expressions.

- "Woo hoo, Jesus, I cannot wait to see how you are going to turn this situation around!"
- "Yippee, I am so excited to see how You, Lord, are going to move in my family, my finances, and my nation!"
- "Father, I am jumping up and down with exhilaration!"
- "I am so excited to see what You are going to do" is the key phrase for delighters. Delighters manifest a childlike faith in God, so let's strengthen our delighting muscles

15

Delighters manifest a childlike faith in God, so let's strengthen our delighting muscles. Also note that delighting is a powerful spiritual weapon. My book, *Crucial Moments*, is a great resource to help you in your delighting journey.

DAY 7
Today is the Day to Be Encouraged

Our ministry's core message affirms the believer's birthright to overflowing hope and joy, and we release strategies for transformational mind renewal to experience the fulfillment and victory that come from right believing. Though many are encouraged by these truths, the process of establishing new strongholds of hope and joy in our minds is a journey that takes time. Just as athletes need to be reminded of their vision and to celebrate progress in the midst of difficult and exhausting training, so do we as we undertake the work to establish new thought patterns and beliefs.

Kris Vallotton often preaches, "Vision gives pain a purpose." In light of this, here are seven reasons for you to overflow with thanksgiving, hope, and joy, even if you are still struggling in your circumstances and emotions:

1. **There is no one like you** – You and your calling are entirely unique and no one can fulfill your purpose like you. There is no one on the planet who is wired and designed just like you, and who has had the exact experiences in life you've had. You can powerfully reach people that few others can.

2. **Many have overcome the challenges you're currently facing** – Whether you're battling personal, relational, financial, or circumstantial obstacles, be encouraged that multitudes

have overcome the same thing and lived a life of purpose and fulfillment.

3. **Your biggest challenge is not about you** – James 1:12 says that a "crown of life" is given to those who overcome. This crown represents authority to impart life and breakthrough to others in the same area which has been overcome. Your greatest struggle right now is equipping you with compassion and power to impart victory and strategies to others for the same battle.

4. **Your past is being turned to good** – "All things work for good for those who love God and are called according to His purpose," (Romans 8:28). As we prioritize our relationship with God, ALL things from our past are working for our good. This is especially encouraging when we consider negative things that have happened in our lives.

5. **You are increasing your load-bearing capacity** – God's purpose is for us to move toward greater kingdom influence in our families, communities, nations, and beyond. In order to have greater influence, we need a greater load-bearing capacity. Both physical and emotional muscles are built by pushing against resistance. Your current difficult circumstances and emotions are opportunities to increase your load-bearing capacity for the great callings on your life in the days ahead.

6. **You are storing up treasure in heaven** – Jesus calls us to do this in Matthew 6:19. As we think from an eternal perspective, we realize that there is much more to life than just having good circumstances here on earth.

7. **God's promises are true** – "Let us hold fast the confession of our hope without wavering, for He who promised is faithful," (Hebrews 10:23). Ultimately, our encouragement comes from believing that God is faithful and His promises are true. As we declare biblical promises, we will be encouraged.

Today is a great day to be encouraged! These seven realities will make a difference for you and those you share them with.

Activation

Declarations:

- I am encouraged today because God's promises are working in my life.
- Because I encourage myself radically, I am able to encourage others in incredible, life-changing ways.
- The truths of this devotional are changing my life.

DAY 8
What Are We Magnifying?

Psalm 34:3 says, "Oh magnify the Lord with me. Let us exalt His name together." It doesn't say, "Oh magnify the problem with me." One of the reasons we get together with other believers is to be in an environment where we magnify (make larger) God in our beliefs and emotions. We can't make God any bigger but we can see Him as bigger. When He gets bigger, our problems get smaller. When we magnify the problem, God gets smaller and the problem gets bigger.

Numbers 13 illustrates this in the story of the twelve spies who go into the promised land. Two of the spies magnified the Lord and came back with the report saying, "We can do this! Let's go up at once!" (When we magnify the Lord, not only do we see Him as bigger, but we see ourselves as bigger too.) The other ten spies magnified the problem instead. They came back and only talked about the problems and challenges. They said, "We are like grasshoppers in our own sight and in their (the giants') sight." When we magnify the problem, not only do we see God as smaller, we see ourselves as smaller too. My question today is this: what are we magnifying?

Here are 7 things we are tempted to magnify instead of the Lord:

1. **The problems we are experiencing** – Sometimes, instead of just sharing the facts about a problem, we can talk ourselves and others right into unbelief. We shouldn't deny the problems (sometimes we need to talk about them), but we cannot regularly

talk about how bad things are. Where there is a lack of hope, there is difficulty in seeing the solutions we actually have.

2. **Our abilities and responsibilities –** We all have responsibilities and important things to do, but when we focus more on what we need to do than what Jesus has done, we magnify ourselves and make God's salvation smaller within our lives. The Gospel is good news. The greater emphasis should always be on the promises and goodness of God.

3. **What the devil is doing** – Certainly, we have an enemy to be wise about, but if we're talking more about Satan's attacks than about God's protection, we magnify the devil more than we are magnifying God (and God then becomes smaller in our eyes). Instead of fighting darkness, spiritual warfare is about turning on the light through exalting what Jesus has done, not what the devil is doing. When the light is on, darkness has to go.

4. **Our past –** There are times when we need to break agreements and tendencies from our family lines, but if we focus more on trying to fix things from the past than focusing on who God says we are as a new creation, then we make God smaller and our weaknesses bigger.

5. **Our apparent disadvantages –** The victim mindset is rooted in the belief that we are at a disadvantage because of _____. It could be our finances, our family, what's going on in our nation, etc. Again, we don't deny those facts, but we can't be fixated on where we feel that we are at a disadvantage from other people. Truly, we all feel disadvantaged in some way. These disadvantages may seemingly hinder things in the short-term, but magnifying God instead brings long-term solutions.

6. **Our feelings –** We don't deny our feelings, but we cannot magnify them above what God has said and Jesus has done. Our feelings are usually indicators of our beliefs. Feelings don't validate truth but what we believe is true. If we want a different emotion, we will need to have a different belief first.

7. **The faults of others** – A perfectionistic, religious perspective creates a critical, fault-finding mindset that thinks poorly of other people. Fixating on what seems to be wrong in others is often a way to justify what is wrong in our own lives. We think, "Well, at least I don't do that." We tend to judge others by their actions but ourselves by our motives. We might magnify what we see wrong with the opposite political party, in leadership over us, in our family, etc. Those things become bigger as we magnify them, and then God seems smaller and hindered by what the people around us are doing.

What are we magnifying? Let's magnify the Lord instead of the problems we're experiencing, our abilities and responsibilities, what the devil is doing, our past, our apparent disadvantages, our feelings, and the apparent faults of others. Let's be like Joshua and Caleb and put our focus on the grace, power, kindness, and goodness of God, and watch Him become magnified in our own lives. Like them, this will help us enter into our Promised Land (and take others with us, too).

DAY 9
Five Reasons to Rejoice Today

In prison, Paul wrote, "Rejoice in the Lord always" (Philippians 4:4). Today is a great day to rejoice and I will share five reasons why below. Before I do, let's look at the three main sources of joy that I have experienced:

1. **Truth joy** – "Now may the God of hope fill you with all joy and peace in believing..." (Romans 15:13). Hope increases with the believing of truth, and it decreases when we renew our minds with lies. "All joy" accompanies this belief-infused hope. We will experience more joy when we increase our godly beliefs.

2. **Holy Spirit joy** – "In His presence is fullness of joy" (Psalm 16:11). I have been in meetings where an outbreak of joy seemingly happens spontaneously, and people become euphoric and laugh uncontrollably. This happened frequently in the 1990s and was termed "Holy Laughter." As with many other God encounters, this Holy Spirit joy can jumpstart us into a joy breakthrough and can shift our theology, so joy is prioritized more highly in the future.

3. **Choosing joy** – "Rejoice in the Lord always, and again I say rejoice." Often I need to tell myself, "Steve, you are going to stir up your joy now. You are going to celebrate and 're-joy' yourself. You need to defeat the discouragement you feel now." This is a necessary part of victorious living.

It is this third source I want to go deeper into today. Here are five reasons that will inspire us to choose joy:

1. **It shifts the atmosphere around us** – We are called to be thermostats, not thermometers. Paul and Silas in Acts 16 were "thermostatic" in prison. They remained spiritually excited in a very difficult situation, and it caused salvation and freedom.

2. **It activates God's promises** – One of the main things to rejoice in is God's promises. When we jubilate in them, we are releasing faith, causing them to manifest in our lives.

3. **It opens our eyes to what we have** – Rejoicing and thanksgiving go hand in hand. Being grateful causes us to see the blessings we already have, and we begin to understand that most of the people in the world would probably want to trade places with us.

4. **It helps us to focus on the eternal** – The greatest thing to rejoice in is the fact that, as followers of Jesus, we have eternal life. If we can find no other joy-igniting truth, then this one is worthy of much emotional celebration.

5. **It is our strength** – Nehemiah 8:10 tells us that the joy of the Lord is our strength. We don't need strength at the end of the battle, but we need it in the middle of the battle – in unresolved situations, uncertainty, and other life challenges. There is no convenient time to radically rejoice, so let's stir it up today.

DAY 10
Reflection, Activation, and Advanced Research on Joy

The discovery of different ways of experiencing joy is a lifelong process. It is always an opportunity to hear from God and receive revelation from Him.

Dr. Pieter Lagaay

Reflection Questions:

1. Which of the four devotionals in this section spoke to you the most and why?
2. What do you believe God is saying to you personally through these devotionals?
3. Who can you encourage today through a voice message, text, phone call, email, or in some other way?

Advanced Research on Joy by Dr. Pieter Lagaay
Joy and the USA's Declaration of Independence

When the Declaration of Independence of the United States was drafted it affirmed a promise that the government would never take away a person's right to life, liberty, and pursuit of happiness. The authors must have understood the power of declarations because this is not only in the title of our country's identity statement but it is also a crucial document included in most legal proceedings. What is even more interesting is that the word "pursuit" was not meant to mean chasing after joy and happiness. As historian Arthur M. Schlesinger explains in a 1964 article in the *William & Mary Quarterly*, titled "The Lost Meaning of 'The Pursuit of Happiness,'" the word "pursuit" should be understood to refer to the same meaning as, "the pursuit of law" or "the pursuit of medicine." That is, pursuit refers to practice or vocation. This means that the framers of the United States Declaration of Independence understood that a person should never be restricted from practicing joy and happiness because it is essential to his/her independence as a person and our identity as a nation!

Just as God gave us life (Genesis 2:7) and liberty (Galatians 5:1), He has also instructed us to practice joy (Philippians 4:4). The framers of the Declaration of Independence demonstrated an understanding of this by affirming that life, liberty, and a person's joy can't be taken away by a government because they have been given by God.

> *"Rejoice in the Lord always. I will say it again: Rejoice!"*
>
> Philippians 4:4

Activation

As you wake up and are getting ready for your day, look at yourself in the mirror and say out loud, "Today, I am practicing joy". While your day goes on, be intentional to ask yourself if you are joyful or joyless. In any area of your day that you feel joyless, make the following declarations:

1. I am not a victim of my circumstances. I am a victor over my circumstances because Christ lives in me!
2. Joy is important in my life and to God. Nothing can rob me of joy because God gave it to me!
3. Even though (state what it is that happened or what it is that is making you feel joyless), I celebrate my progress, not my perfection. So I will never stop practicing being joyful!

DAY 11
The Culture of Gladness

"For the kingdom of God is not eating and drinking, but righteousness and peace and joy in the Holy Spirit"
(Romans 14:17).

As I mentioned before, when I first heard someone say that joy was one-third of the Kingdom, I thought to myself, "I don't think so. It cannot not be that important." Since then, I have become convinced it actually is.

I believe righteousness, peace, and joy are each one-third of the Kingdom. If we get those right, we will get the Kingdom right.

As we focus on righteousness, we will:

- Understand the gospel of grace and reign in life (Romans 5:17)
- Get our identity established because we will know we are the righteousness of God in Christ (2 Corinthians 5:21)
- Recognize that our belief we are righteous is the main key to manifesting righteous behavior (John 8:31-32)
- See unrighteous behavior and attitudes as a sign of a disconnection in our relationship with God, not as something we should be punished for (Galatians 5:22-23)

As we focus our attention on peace, we will:

- Increase our trust in God and overcome worry (Philippians 4:6-7)
- Prioritize healthy and loving relationships (Romans 12:18)
- Have confidence in our relationship with God (Romans 5:1)

With that said, this devotional is about the "joy third" of the kingdom. As I emphasize this, I want to highlight three verses in the Bible. They are three of many, but these have especially spoken to me recently.

The Culture of Gladness Verse – "Your God, has anointed You (Jesus) with the oil of gladness more than Your companions" (Hebrews 1:9). The context of this verse is about Jesus loving righteousness and hating wickedness which are the main emphases under the Old Covenant law, and this was the reason He was anointed with the oil of gladness above all others. Because of our faith in Christ's perfect obedience for us, we too are anointed with oil of gladness. This contributed to my belief joy is one-third of the Kingdom because:

- Great leaders (including parents) establish a culture of gladness around them. To do this, they must defeat unworthiness, controlling others, fear of punishment, manipulation, and a whole host of other non-Kingdom advancing mindsets.
- Gladness includes laughter. I have a difficult time trusting the perspective of any leader who does not value laughter. Laughter is not the only component of the culture of gladness (and I recognize we don't laugh all the time), but it is an important one. Again, to laugh, we have to let go of something, and letting go of those "somethings" is important for healthy kingdom increase.

The "Serving the Lord With Gladness" Verse – "Make a joyful shout to the Lord, all you lands! Serve the Lord with gladness" (Psalms 100:1-2). I believe when we have consistently let go of gladness in our commitments, responsibilities, or assignments, then we have most likely hit the lid of our influence and kingdom increase. When we pursue serving the Lord with gladness, we will:

- Realize there is no convenient time to be radically joyful. There is seemingly always a reason why now is not a good time to be joyful. I used to unconsciously believe there would come a day when everything would be lined up for my joy (no personal weaknesses, no financial needs, no relational challenges, no uncertainties for the future, and no negative news in the media). That was a delusion.
- Understand faithfulness is not just showing up, but how we think when we show up. We show up full of faith, and I believe gladness is one of the fruits of faith. We cannot wait for a better time to bring ourselves fully and enthusiastically to the places and people we are called to. We all have things in our current assignments we do not like. As we push against this resistance with gladness, we will build our joy muscles.
- Recognize regular gladness is one of the signs we have passed the tests at the level we are in, and we are ready for promotion and more of the kingdom.

The "Being a Cheerful Decider" Verse – "So let each one give as he purposes in his heart, not grudgingly or of necessity; for God loves a cheerful giver" (2 Corinthians 9:7). This verse empowers us to develop a good decision making process and then attach faith to those decisions (purposes in our hearts). As I have meditated on this verse, I have reached these conclusions which further strengthen my belief that joy is one-third of the kingdom.

- Cheerfulness is one of the main evidences we have attached faith to our decisions.
- Any responsibility, commitment, or assignment that I do not have cheerfulness in is most likely an indicator I have not attached faith to doing it. This could be ministry assignments, meetings I attend, my marriage, bills I pay, or mowing the grass.
- Declarations are a powerful way to attach faith to what I am doing or will do. When I speak out loud, "This is going to be a great meeting," energy, power, and cheerfulness start to bubble up in me.

Is joy one-third of the kingdom? Do great influencers prioritize the creation of a culture of gladness? I believe so. When we pursue joy:

- We will be compelled to overcome the real enemies of the Kingdom (victim mindsets, pessimism, fear, unworthiness, insignificance, etc.)
- We will need to deal with the doubt and double mindedness fueling our lack of attaching faith to our assignments, responsibilities, and commitments.
- We will be led to create an environment that people will want to be a part of and will thrive in.

Let's go for it and create a greater culture of gladness in and around us. We (and others) won't be sorry.

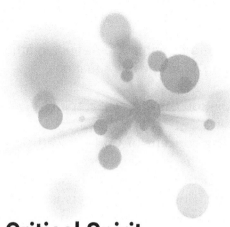

DAY 12
Defeating the Critical Spirit

Joyfulness and a critical spirit cannot coexist. A "critical spirit" is a compulsive attitude of criticism and fault-finding, which tears down others rather than building them up. It is at the heart of what Jesus spoke of in Matthew seven.

> "Judge not, that you be not judged. For with what judgment you judge, you will be judged; and with the measure you use, it will be measured back to you. And why do you look at the speck in your brother's eye, but do not consider the plank in your own eye? Or how can you say to your brother, 'Let me remove the speck from your eye'; and look, a plank is in your own eye? Hypocrite! First remove the plank from your own eye, and then you will see clearly to remove the speck from your brother's eye."
>
> (Matthew 7:1-5)

This is an incredible passage that warns of the negative consequences of fault-finding, and it also gives one of the cures for the critical spirit: focusing on our own growth when tempted to judge others negatively.

Destructive criticism is different from constructive feedback. The only criticism that is ever constructive is that which speaks the truth in love and wants to help the person become all that they are meant to be.

Again, the critical spirit is a fault-finding attitude, and it primarily sees what is wrong in people and situations.

What are the sources of a critical spirit?

- **Faulty concept of God** – If we believe God loves us but does not like us, we will project this belief onto others.
- **Self-criticism** – We "love our neighbor as ourselves" (Mark 12:31). How we treat others is largely determined by how we treat ourselves. If we are focused mainly on our faults, we will tend to look for faults in others.
- **Perfectionist attitude** – Perfectionists only celebrate and become joyful when there is perfection in others and themselves.
- **Self-justification** – People often use the sins and faults of others to justify their own wrong behaviors.
- **Pride** – Pride causes us to use the faults of others to make ourselves feel superior.

Why is the critical spirit a problem?

- **It is partnering with the devil instead of God** – The devil is "the accuser of the brethren" (Revelation 12:10).
- **It limits our influence** – It is difficult to influence those we do not love or have hope for.
- **It leads to speaking death instead of life** – What we believe in our hearts will come out in words (Matthew 12:34).
- **It causes others to criticize us** – "Judge not, that you be not judged. For with what judgment you judge, you will be judged; and with the measure you use, it will be measured back to you." (Matthew 7:1)
- **It limits our ability to experience joy and abundance** – Having a regularly critical attitude is a sign of a non-prosperous soul. "Beloved, I pray that you may prosper in all things and be in health, just as your soul prospers." (3 John 2)
- **It greatly limits our ability to restore others** – "Brethren, if a man is overtaken in any trespass, you who are spiritual restore such a one in a spirit of gentleness, considering yourself lest you

also be tempted." (Galatians 6:1) In this verse, fault finders are not considered spiritual.

How to defeat this spirit

- **Prioritize love** – 1 Corinthians 13 tells us if we do seemingly great kingdom things but treat people poorly in our actions and thoughts, it profits nothing. And the kind of love mentioned in this chapter demolishes the critical spirit. "Love suffers long and is kind; love does not envy; love does not parade itself, is not puffed up; does not behave rudely, does not seek its own, is not provoked, thinks no evil; does not rejoice in iniquity, but rejoices in the truth; bears all things, believes all things, hopes all things, endures all things." (vs 4-7)
- **Get a father mindset instead of an elder brother mindset** – The elder brother in the story of the prodigal son (Luke 15) is the poster child for the critical spirit. In contrast to his father, he criticizes his brother (and his father too). The default of the elder-brother mindset is to first see what is wrong with a person or place. The default of the father-mindset is to first see what is right with a person or place.
- **Take the plank out of your eye** – We will stop criticizing others if we turn every opportunity to criticize into a time of personal growth for ourselves. As we do this, we will see clearly to really help others get rid of the speck in their eye.
- **Pray for those you are tempted to criticize** – When we immediately pray for those we want to criticize, then we invest into their future and become part of the solution rather than being part of the problem.

Let's read these words of Jesus again: "Judge not, that you be not judged. For with what judgment you judge, you will be judged; and with the measure you use, it will be measured back to you."

I am not saying we should never confront wrong behavior or set strong boundaries in our relationships, but I am saying that having a critical spirit will bring unnecessary damage to ourselves and others. This message is needed always but especially now with so many negatively labeling anyone who disagrees with them.

Let's become part of the solution and defeat the critical spirit in our lives, families, and organizations. This will help us greatly to walk in personal joy and create a culture of gladness around us.

DAY 13
My Joy is Not Another's Responsibility

"To laugh you have to let go of something." I frequently say this when introducing the concept of laughing at lies. I go on to say, "Wendy and I have been married for over forty years. We love each other and are best friends, but even so, we don't always agree with each other. Ha ha. And, when I think she is really wrong, I am not laughing. Because if I laugh, then she will think things are okay. I don't want her to think that. I am tempted to say, 'I am a victim of you. My joy depends on your behavior. For me to walk in biblical joy, I need you to do what I think you should do.' (Ha ha.) But how many of you know when I laugh with her, I have let go of that thing (whether it was anger, manipulation, frustration, or whatever). You cannot hold on to those things and laugh at the same time. You have to let go of one or the other. Now I know we don't laugh all the time. We 'weep with those who weep' (Romans 12:15), and when we are having brave communication with people we are usually not laughing, but laughter is still a powerful and needed weapon in the mouths of believers. Yes, to laugh, you must let go of something."

I chuckle every time I share this, especially when I indicate my joy levels depend on Wendy's behavior. I laugh, but I am also convicted because I realize how much I DO depend on what other people do to determine my level of joy.

One of the biggest lies of the victim mindset is this: Other people are responsible for my joy level and happiness. If we believe this, we are unconsciously looking for a spouse, our children, our parents,

35

a friend, a leader, or someone else to do the right thing to prove they love us, to validate us, or to make us happy.

Hear this: we cannot depend on other people to fill our joy tank. Ultimately, every person will disappoint us in some way. If we depend on others and don't take responsibility for it ourselves, then we will never find the joy of the Lord as our strength.

Codependency in our relationships causes us to primarily look to others to meet our emotional needs. *Codependency is characterized by a person belonging to a dysfunctional, one-sided relationship where one person relies on the other for meeting nearly all of their emotional and self-esteem needs. It also describes a relationship that enables another person to maintain their irresponsible, addictive, or underachieving behavior.* (Quoted from Psych Central website).

Here are six steps to take to break the tendency of expecting others to meet our self-esteem and emotional needs (including our joy):

1. **Admit our tendencies** – It is a forward-moving act to humble ourselves and admit our dependence on others for our joy level.

2. **Repent from it** – As we humble ourselves before God, we will find grace to renounce and replace this victim mindset with the truth that we are strong and powerful in Him (and that we are not a victim but a victor).

3. **Take ownership of your own joy** – Say this out loud: "I, not others, determine how much joy I walk in."

4. **Value soul prosperity over good circumstances** – Our response to something is almost always more important than the something. "Beloved, I pray that you be in health and prosper in all things, even as your soul prospers" (3 John 2).

5. **Get vision and purpose for difficult times** – "My brethren, count it all joy when you fall into various trials, knowing . . ." (James 1:2-3). We build our joy muscle by pushing against

negative emotions with the promises of God in our thoughts and words.

6. **Celebrate progress, not perfection** – It is one thing to take ownership of our own joy, but it is a real journey to walk it out. Just as a toddler does not walk perfectly at first, we too will not walk perfectly at first as we take ownership of our joy. To combat the lie, "I cannot do this," we celebrate progress instead of perfection.

Activation

Truly, to laugh we have to let go of something. Let's laugh and release others from the responsibility of keeping us joyful and happy. As we do, it will be amazing how this will actually cause us to increase our ability to bring joy to others (especially those who are closest to us).

DAY 14
Spiritual Rest

If God wants people to like me, they will.

Wendy Backlund

"For we who have believed do enter that rest..."

(Hebrews 4:3).

"There remains therefore a rest for the people of God. For he who has entered His rest has himself also ceased from his works as God did from His"

(Hebrews 4:9-10).

"Let us therefore be diligent to enter that rest..."

(Hebrews 4:11).

I believe Hebrews 4 is one of the seventeen most important chapters in the Bible (the others would be Galatians 1-6, Ephesians 1-3, Colossians 1-2, and Romans 4-8). I believe if we get these chapters deep in us, it will be the key for us to interpret the rest of the Bible in a healthy and accurate way.

Hebrews 4 is the spiritual rest chapter. This rest is not necessarily a ceasing from activity (although the sabbath principle of resting is a good thing), but it is a mindset of trusting God which causes a deep peace. Inactivity alone, without true spiritual rest obtained from God, results in trying to relax with a lack of peace. But those resting in the

Father's love and provision can experience deep peace and refreshment even while being active and busy.

My wife, Wendy, has influenced me much to value spiritual rest. Unlike her, I tend to be driven to achieve and have some work-a-holic tendencies in me. (Let's just laugh at that.) Her insights have helped me experience more godly rest.

She has influenced me to develop these five beliefs to walk in Hebrews 4 spiritual rest:

1. **The Favor Belief** – Wendy says, "If God wants people to like me, they will." In other words, whoever I am meant to have favor with, I will. Yes, there are things we can do to increase the likelihood of having favor (being honest, treating people well, being skilled, etc.), but ultimately we can rest in trusting God for the doors He wants to have open for us.

2. **The Anointing Belief** – When Wendy was struggling with being able to speak in front of others, she heard Bill Johnson say, "There is coming such a powerful revival that all you will need to say is 'peanut butter' and people will say, 'What must I do to be saved?'" Wendy thought, "I can say Peanut butter." She realized her faith was not meant to be in the words she spoke, but in God's ability to anoint what she said. This has brought her so much freedom and given her rest in public speaking, in one-on-one conversations, and in counseling others.

3. **The Peace Belief** – "You have authority over any storm you can sleep in" – Bill Johnson. I love this quote, and it goes along with something Wendy says. "Peace is one of our greatest weapons in prayer." Before we pray about a situation, it is important to overcome fear and worry before actually praying about it. If you have 30-minutes for prayer, spend 25 minutes in worship, biblical meditation, magnifying the Lord, and praying in the Spirit so that your heart is at peace; then use the last five minutes to pray about the situation.

4. **The Mark 11:24 Belief** – "Therefore I say to you, whatever things you ask when you pray, believe that you receive them, and you will have them" (Mark 11:24). We first receive in our spirits the promises of God, answers to prayer, and our biblical identity before they manifest in our lives. What key area of your life have you already received the answer in your spirit? Why don't you note the date you received it, and regularly declare, "On _____(date) I received _____. I am excited to see it manifest in my life." This will help you walk in spiritual rest concerning this aspect of your life.

5. **The "God is for Me" Belief** – Wendy heard this from the Lord, "I don't want to wait for you to be perfect before using you." Look at the last two verses from Hebrews 4. "For we do not have a High Priest who cannot sympathize with our weaknesses, but was in all points tempted as we are, yet without sin. Let us therefore come boldly to the throne of grace, that we may obtain mercy and find grace to help in time of need" (Hebrews 4:15-16). As we consider our personal weaknesses, we can have spiritual rest because we know God understands us and is providing grace and help to us. He is really for you. (This song will help convince you of that – The Blessing with Kari Jobe & Cody Carnes | Live From Elevation Ballantyne | Elevation Worship)

Spiritual rest is a needed foundation for joy to manifest in us.

DAY 15
Reflection, Activation, and Advanced Research on Joy

Resolve to keep happy and your joy shall form an invincible host against difficulties.

Helen Keller Reflection questions:

1. Which of the four devotionals in this section spoke to you the most and why?
2. What do you believe God is saying to you personally through these devotionals?
3. Who can you encourage today through a voice message, text, phone call, email, or in some other way?

Advanced Research on Joy by Dr. Pieter Lagaay
Joy and Epigenetics

Believing we can have joy in our lives is more of a physiological reality than we think. Statements we have heard like "This is just how I am", or "It just runs in my family" may feel true but are pathological beliefs that are biochemically incorrect. Epigenetics is the scientific explanation that explains why.

Epigenetics means something other than genetics. When we make statements like those above, we are leaving out the word "epi" in "epigenetics". The genetic part of epigenetics is the automatic unique genetic sequence of our DNA strands. Each DNA strand has a very unique arrangement of DNA molecules. Portions of the DNA strand will code or translate as a gene, and, generally speaking, the order of our DNA molecules on the strand does not change. That's the fundamental basis of genetics. But when we add the word "epi" we are saying there is an added factor that influences how our unique DNA sequence is coded or translated.

For example, you may have a code in your DNA strand for anxiety, depression, and joy. Just because you have that code, it doesn't mean you will experience anxiety, depression, and joy. The question is, "How are these emotions turned on or off?" Epigenetics explains the answer to how our code is read. It's what you believe. If you believe that you are a victim of circumstances then you will turn on that code and various chemicals will be released that affect the synapses in your brain to make you feel depressed or anxious. If, however, you believe Philippians 4:6-7 and declare this over your life, you will change how your DNA is translated and change the translation of your genetic code. Instead of turning on the code for depression and anxiety, they will be turned off and joy will be turned on!

"Do not be anxious about anything, but in every situation, by prayer and petition, with thanksgiving, present your requests to God. And the peace of God, which transcends all understanding, will guard your hearts and your minds in Christ Jesus." Philippians 4:6-7

Activation

Turning your "Epi-" on. Every day for 4 weeks make these declarations when you wake up, have lunch, and before you go to dinner.

- I am turning on my genes for a positive attitude.
- I am turning on my genes to laugh.
- I am turning off my complaining genes.

Find a friend, family member, or co-worker who is not experiencing joy. Be the word "epi" in epigenetics and encourage them about what they are believing in a situation. Spend time listening and not fixing what is turned on or off. Be the light of encouragement that speaks life into them, especially if it is something you can identify with. Declare a positive belief that you are struggling the most to believe over someone else and attach the highest level of faith you can to it. Then tell this person "God is doing it through you right now!"

DAY 16
You Already Have It

The Prophet Elisha asked the widow who was in a crisis of debt, "What do you have?" She said, "I have nothing, except a little oil."

One of the main purposes of prophetic ministry is to cause us to take our eyes off what we think we don't have to actually see what we do have. This is what happened to the widow.

You can read the whole story about Elisha and this widow in 2 Kings 4:1-7. It is a good one. It tells us that one of the sons of the prophets died and left a widow behind. She was in debt and the creditors wanted to take her children as payment. She asked Elisha for help. He asked her what she had in her house. She said she had a little oil and it became the source of an astounding miracle of debt cancellation and future provision.

The widow started her answer with, "I have nothing." The enemy of our souls wants us to constantly focus on what we think we don't have as we contemplate a problem or think about our future. The lies he spews often use negative comparisons with others to try to convince us that we are at a disadvantage in life. He tempts us to believe we have nothing or too little to see significant positive change:

- Not enough intelligence
- Not enough good looks

- Not enough money
- Not enough love for God
- Not enough favor with key people
- Not enough physical strength

People ready to go to the next level do not fixate on:

- Their weaknesses
- What is missing from their lives
- What went wrong in the past
- What they think they should be

I am not saying we ignore our weaknesses or the pain we have experienced, but the widow moved past it and had this revelation: "I already have it! I have everything I need for the miracle to happen."

Let me give you a "now" word for your life: You already have what you need to see the miracle, to see forward movement, to get out of the bondage of debt, and to be a radical, positive influence. As you identify and attach faith to the advantages you have and the skills/giftings you have, it will bring a turnaround and increase.

Peter told the lame man, "Silver or gold I do not have, but what I do have I give you" (Acts 3:6). Peter did not walk in false-humility, believing he had nothing. No, he identified that he had power to bring healing to the physically afflicted.

So, what do you have? What are you good at? What advantages do you have? Examples of these could be:

- I am good at listening
- I am good at bouncing back from adversity
- I have a gift of encouragement
- I have a good job
- I have a home and a car
- I have a good sense of humor
- I have the advantage of living in the nation I live in

- I have the promises of God
- I am who God says I am
- I am a good cook

Activation

Why don't you make your own list? Once you get started, the list will get quite lengthy (longer than you probably thought). Each thing you list has unlimited potential in it. It certainly was true with the widow's oil. Consider how her story unfolded.

After the widow said she had a little oil, "Elisha said, 'Go around and ask all your neighbors for empty jars. Don't ask for just a few. Then go inside and shut the door behind you and your sons. Pour oil into all the jars, and as each is filled, put it to one side.' . . .When all the jars were full, she said to her son, 'Bring me another one.' But he replied, 'There is not a jar left.' Then the oil stopped flowing" (2 Kings 4:3-6).

I propose as we identify what we have, attach faith to its significance, and then dedicate it to the glory of God, the supernatural oil of provision and power will keep flowing. Something incredible happens when we say, "Father, I dedicate my gift of encouragement to your glory and to the breakthrough of others. I dedicate my house, my ability to listen, my favor, my cooking ability, my carpentry skill, and my healing anointing to you and the benefit of other people. Such as I have, I will give to bless You and others."

Woo hoo!! You already have it. You are seeing it like never before. You are going to see the oil keep flowing to you and through you. Say out loud with me: "I already have it!"

DAY 17
That's It! That's the Stronghold!

In the first week of serving at one of the churches I pastored, someone told me, "This city is hard for the gospel." I thought, "That's it!" Agreement with negative past experience creates a stronghold! I knew if I believed that my city was hard for the gospel, I would be the biggest problem in the city. In essence, my beliefs would be the biggest stronghold hindering God's will.

What do you think are the greatest strongholds blocking the purposes of God? Are they demonic, regional principalities? Are they people possessed by the devil? While we don't discount our wrestling against the principalities and powers mentioned in Ephesians 6:12, they are not the root problem. In reality, the only thing that can really hinder the will of God is what we believe. The greatest strongholds that we wrestle with are in our minds.

2 Corinthians 10:4-5 is the most quoted spiritual warfare passage in the Bible. It does not mention the devil, but highlights the need to aggressively control our thinking. "For the weapons of our warfare are not carnal but mighty in God for pulling down strongholds, casting down arguments and every high thing that exalts itself against the knowledge of God, bringing every thought into captivity to the obedience of Christ." The highest level of spiritual warfare is the decision to believe and think higher than what we are experiencing and feeling.

2 Corinthians 10:4 says we are empowered to pull down strongholds with supernatural weapons. A stronghold is a place that has been fortified to protect it against attack. A stronghold in our thinking is created by repetitive agreement with a belief. It is called a stronghold because it has a strong hold. It will defend its right to be in our thinking. It must be pulled down, demolished, and taken captive (2 Corinthians 10:4-5).

We are called to "cast down arguments". Our feelings and past experiences want to argue with what God says is true. Moses, Abraham, Sarah, Gideon, and a whole host of Bible characters argued with God concerning who He said they were and what He said they could do.

The greatest strongholds blocking the purposes of God are created by Christians agreeing with their feelings and past experiences. We don't deny the past; we just don't get our beliefs from it. We don't deny it has been hard, but we should not name it "hard". If we do, then that's the stronghold. That's it! That is what is blocking God's purposes.

In talking about what the real strongholds are, I do not want to give the impression that we should ignore the devil. I am grateful for those who have powerful deliverance ministries and who help us do what Jesus did as shown in Acts 10:38: "How God anointed Jesus of Nazareth with the Holy Spirit and with power, who went about doing good and healing all who were oppressed by the devil, for God was with Him." But I believe we have greatly overemphasized the devil and underemphasized our beliefs when talking about spiritual warfare.

We are not to call things by their past, but we are to call them by God's promises. "God, who gives life to the dead and calls those things which do not exist as though they did" (Romans 4:17). This is illustrated in Joel 3:10: "Let the weak say, 'I am strong.'" If we are battling weakness, we may need medicine, doctors, or counseling, but even so, we still believe we are strong. If we call ourselves weak, then that is the stronghold that will work against all the other things we are trying to do to overcome our weakness.

So, what argument of past experience has or is trying to create a self-limiting stronghold in your life? What arguments against God's truth are coming out of your mouth? There is grace available to you now to demolish these arguments like never before.

Finally, in Judges 6, the nation of Israel and the people of God were in a very dark time. They were oppressed by an unwelcome, oppressive governmental system of the Midianites. In that seemingly hopeless situation, God spoke hope to a man named Gideon. He argued at first but eventually came to a place of being fully convinced about what God was saying and about saving his nation. What's fascinating about this is that the stronghold blocking God's purposes was not the Midianites (negative government over them), Baal worship (a backslidden people), or a demonic principality; but it was in Gideon's thinking. The future of the nation of Israel was locked up in Gideon's thinking. Once he thought right, the nation was saved.

"Gideon, that's it! That lie in your thinking is the stronghold! It's coming down and it will bring national revival."

Friends, we are the Gideons of our time. Nations will be saved as we change how we think.

DAY 18
A Different Kind of Repenting

"Lord, I am so sorry and I'm grieving that I am not believing I am righteous, and I repent of that right now."

"Everyone who has been believing lies about God, others, your circumstances, or about yourself, run to the altar right now and repent."

"Please do not participate in communion until you have repented of the belief you are not 100% worthy to do so through Jesus' obedience and death on the cross."

These statements are not the norm in how we think, but should they be? I say, "yes," because the Greek meaning of the word repentance is "to change the way you think".

I am so looking forward to when there are powerful repentance meetings where people will repent like this: 1) "Lord, I am so sorry that I have believed that I am who my past says I am and not who You say I am." 2) "Father, I am so sorry that I have not believed You love me unconditionally." 3) "Lord, I am grieved that I have believed that I am a sinner instead of a saint." 4) "Father, I am experiencing deep Godly sorrow because I have believed I am unworthy to be blessed."

I do not want to devalue the importance of repenting from wrong behaviors, but the greatest thing to repent from is believing lies. 1 Corinthians 10:13 says, "No temptation has come upon you except which is common to man . . ." The most dangerous temptations we face are to believe lies. The devil is the father of all lies (John 8:44). He is only empowered when we meditate on and believe his falsehoods. This is what happened to Eve in the garden in Genesis 3. She was first deceived about God's character and then sinned in her actions. We all hear the same lies that we need to repent from.

When I heard Francis Frangipane say, "Every area of your life that doesn't glisten with hope means you're believing a lie and that area is a stronghold of the devil in your life", I realized that my greatest repentance was going to be about lies that I was believing. And this repentance was not a one-time event. I realized I was not done repenting until I had glistening hope in the area that I was repenting about.

Repentance is indeed a lifestyle, not an event. I am to daily and intentionally change the way I think (repent). I am transformed by the renewing of my mind. The renewing of the mind could also be called repentance. I am transformed by the repenting in my mind (my thoughts).

Again, there is a place for deep sorrow for the wrong behaviors we have (see 2 Corinthians 7:8-12), but this sorrow needs to lead us to confront the beliefs producing the behaviors.

Let's get back to the idea of a different kind of repentance meeting. One place it can happen is during our communion services. "Therefore whoever eats this bread or drinks this cup of the Lord in an unworthy manner will be guilty of the body and blood of the Lord. But let a man examine himself, and so let him eat of the bread and drink of the cup. For he who eats and drinks in an unworthy manner eats and drinks judgment to himself, not discerning the Lord's body. For this reason many are weak and sick among you, and many sleep" (1 Corinthians 11:27-30).

"Let a man examine himself." For most of my life, during communion, I have examined my behavior, not my beliefs. I found myself believing I was taking communion in an "unworthy manner" if I did not measure up behaviorally. Certainly, if we are not sincere about our relationship with Jesus, it is unwise to participate in communion, but I would argue we are taking communion in an unworthy manner if we do not believe Jesus has made us fully worthy to participate in it. Space does not allow for an exhaustive study on this, but I invite you to pray into what I am sharing.

Finally, the key to repentance is valuing and immersing ourselves in God's Word.

It will actually cause us to let go of lies and believe truth:

- **Abide in the Word, know truth, be made free** – "Then Jesus said to those Jews who believed Him, 'If you abide in My word, you are My disciples indeed. And you shall know the truth, and the truth shall make you free'" (John 8:32).
- **Word in our heart prevents sin** – "Your word I have hidden in my heart, that I might not sin against You" (Psalm 119:11).
- **The Word in us saves our souls (our mind, will, and emotions)** – "Receive with meekness the implanted word, which is able to save your souls" (James 1:21).
- **Get the Word in our mouths and it will cause obedience, prosperity, and success** – "This Book of the Law shall not depart from your mouth, but you shall meditate in it day and night, that you may observe to do according to all that is written in it. For then you will make your way prosperous, and then you will have good success" (Joshua 1:8).

How about having a different kind of repentance meeting? Many of you already do this but may not have realized it. Let's truly make it a lifestyle to repent and not quit until we have glistening hope in the area we are repenting of. (And it is exciting to know joy will come with this glistening hope.)

DAY 19
"My Laughter Feels Fake"

"A merry heart does good, like medicine"
(Proverbs 17:22).

I remember being uncomfortable with speakers who asked me to laugh. It felt fake and inauthentic to laugh when I didn't feel like it. Judging by the awkward and hesitant laughter I felt from others in the room at the time, I was not alone in my discomfort. Over time, I've changed my view on the subject. Here's why:

Laughter is one of the main expressions of a merry, cheerful heart. I love finding ways to consistently activate the discipline of laughter because:

- **Medical research has proven the health benefits of laughter** – We reference this in this book. Also, if you do an online search for laughter and health benefits, you will find fascinating studies inspiring you to laugh.
- **Laughter helps us to "let go" of negative mindsets** – Whether it is frustration, pessimism, unworthiness, discouragement, or something else, laughter can be a powerful tool to help us let go of these self-limiting belief systems. Why? Because you cannot hold on to them and laugh at the same time.
- **Laughter disempowers lies** – "He who sits in the heavens laughs" (Psalms 2:4). The context of this verse indicates God is laughing at what His enemies are saying and planning. When

we can join God and laugh at the lies restricting us, we take a major step toward loosening their grip on us.

- **Laughter is key to healthy families, organizations, and relationships in general** – "Jesus was anointed with the oil of gladness above all His companions" (Hebrews 1:9). Jesus brought gladness into His relationships while on earth. Those who laugh together tend to stay together.

By now you may be thinking "Okay, Steve, we see that laughter is important, but how about authenticity? Isn't it inauthentic to laugh when we don't feel like it?"

Please consider this question with me: if you go to the gym to work out when you don't feel like working out, is it a fake workout? Are the physical benefits you see from weightlifting canceled out because your emotions weren't on board?

If you read your Bible when you don't feel like it, is it fake Bible reading? If you go to church when you don't feel like it, is it fake church attendance? If you still act lovingly toward your family when you don't feel loving, is it fake love?

Obviously the answer is no. These are all habits we intentionally develop and maintain for successful living. Part of maturing is learning to do what's right and good for us even—and especially—when we don't feel like doing it. Just as our feelings are not our primary barometer of truth, authenticity is more about our behavior lining up with our values, not with how we may feel.

I believe valuing and practicing regular laughter is a vital habit to be developed and maintained for a healthy life and healthy relationships. As we implement it and work out our laughter muscles, it will become easier, and our feelings will naturally start to become more positive about the practice. Just as positive fitness results can motivate and spur us on to higher levels of physical challenge and enjoyment, once we begin to see the positive effects of laughter on our lives, we will start to get excited about the results we see in our mindsets, relationships, and general outlook. What might happen if you took the leap? What begins feeling fake for you might just change your life for the better. It has for me.

DAY 20
Reflection, Activation, and Advanced Research on Joy

Reflection questions:

1. Which of the four devotionals in this section spoke to you the most and why?
2. What do you believe God is saying to you personally through these devotionals?
3. Who can you encourage today through a voice message, text, phone call, email, or in some other way?

Advanced Research on Joy by Dr. Pieter Lagaay
Health Benefits of Laughter

Norman Cousins's book, *Anatomy of an Illness* published in 1979, was one of the first publications to document laughter as creating an analgesic effect for pain. Since Cousin's book, scientific research and the therapeutic effects of laughter have grown. A randomized controlled study showed that laughter reduces anxiety and insomnia and resulted in an improvement in general health. Since this study, the science of laughter revealed two types of laughter: spontaneous and self-induced. This begs the question; Are the health benefits of laughter dependent on the type of laughter we experience?

The Motion Creates Emotion Theory (MCET) has shown that **our bodies don't know the difference between intentionally laughing and laughing instinctively**. When we make ourselves laugh we experience the same physiologic health benefits as when we experience spontaneous laughter!

In 2020 another randomized controlled study demonstrated the healing effect of laughter in patients with schizophrenia. This study demonstrated that when people intentionally laugh, a protein in the brain called brain-derived neurotrophic factor (BNDF) and cortisol increase. BDNF is responsible for brain cell growth and neuronal plasticity. Neuronal plasticity helps people with their ability to learn and increase their memory.

Whether we laugh in response to something or we make ourselves laugh, the effects on our health are nothing but positive. Solomon seemed to recognize the health benefits when he said that "a merry heart does good like medicine" (Proverbs 17:22). The Hebrew word used for merry is *a Sameah* which is a verb for showing joy, rejoicing, or being gleeful. Like Solomon, science has come to understand that laughing is more than just a response to a positive emotion, but it actually heals.

Activation

At the beginning of the week start by exercising your "laugher" by not just laughing in response to humor but also by intentionally laughing. Every day for one week find 5 things to laugh at/about. It can be lies that you are believing or it can just be choosing to laugh at a joke even when you don't feel like it. Either way, exercise your "laugher". Here are some other ideas:

- **Play the smiley game** – With two or more people, see who can look at each other the longest without smiling.
- **Watch funny dog videos** – Famous marriage and family counselor (and talk show host), Dr. Laura Schlessinger recommends doing this each evening before going to bed to reduce stress and stir up joy.

- **Share short (clean) jokes with your family and with other groups** – Laughter has an unusual ability to bond people together.
- **Laugh for one minute non-stop** – you can do this by yourself or with others.

After the week is over take inventory and assess any improvement in physical pain that you have had, difficulty sleeping, or anxiety. Share your testimony with Igniting Hope at info@ignitinghope.com and continue to implement exercising your "laughter" daily.

DAY 21
Thanksgiving is a Gateway to Joy

"The weapons we fight with . . .have divine power to demolish strongholds. We demolish arguments and every high thing that sets itself up against the knowledge of God, and we take captive every thought to make it obedient to Christ"

(2 Corinthians 10:4-5).

This is the most quoted spiritual warfare passage in the Bible. It is not talking about regional demonic strongholds but about strongholds in our own thinking. The highest level of spiritual warfare is to change the way we think – to demolish the arguments of negative experience and negative feelings with God's promises and our new creation identity (2 Peter 1:4; 2 Corinthians 5:17).

We are told we have supernatural weapons available to us to defeat self-limiting and problem-causing thinking patterns. It does not say "weapon" but "weapons." As we mature in our faith, we will identify and activate what God has provided for us to be victorious. Here are some of the weapons of warfare I have discovered.

- **The Word of God** – "Take . . .the sword of the Spirit which is the word of God" (Ephesians 6:17). We fight and defeat lies with what we believe God has said to us.
- **Laughing at lies** – "He who sits in the heavens laughs" (Psalms 2:4). The context of this is that God is laughing at what His

enemies are saying and planning. When we can laugh at the lies creating our negative strongholds, we start to disempower them.

- **Forgiveness** – "Father, forgive them" (Luke 23:34). Believing in God's forgiveness for us is a major door to demolish lies of orphanhood and unworthiness. Also, our forgiveness for others brings a spiritual freedom to those we forgive.
- **Faith declarations** – "God, who gives life to the dead and calls those things which do not exist as though they did" (Romans 4:17). As we declare God's truth over the seeming dead areas in and around us, we weaken the strongholds supporting the lack of life.

There are more weapons, including experiencing God's love and experiencing supernatural deliverance from an anointed person, but I want to spend the remaining time speaking about the powerful weapon of "thank you."

In my devotional book Victorious Mindsets, I have fifty beliefs to intentionally speak and believe. One of the devotions is "I Am Thankful to God and People." I speak there about my theory that "thank you" might be the most powerful words we speak. It is indeed one of the best weapons to demolish strongholds. **Here are three reasons why I believe this:**

1. **"Thank you" is a principal way to take our thoughts captive** – "We take captive every thought to make it obedient to Christ." It is the key for staying in faith and out of worry. "Be anxious for nothing, but in everything by prayer and supplication, with thanksgiving, let your requests be made known to God; and the peace of God, which surpasses all understanding, will guard your hearts and minds through Christ Jesus" (Philippians 4:6-7). When we are tempted to worry, we can capture the negative thought through thanksgiving. "Thank you, Father, you are meeting this need. Thank you for moving in my loved one's life. Thank you for healing my body."

2. **"Thank you" is part of delighting in the Lord and seeing our desires fulfilled** – "Delight yourself also in the Lord, and He shall give you the desires of your heart" (Psalms 37:4). As we focus on what we have, rather than what it seems we don't have, we take the first step into a radical delighting that will cause us to experience our deepest desires. Thanksgiving is both a cause and an evidence of soul prosperity. "Beloved, I pray that you may prosper in all things and be in health, just as your soul prospers" (3 John 2).

3. **"Thank you" gets us unstuck and moving forward into new seasons and dimensions of life** – "Enter into His gates with thanksgiving, and into His courts with praise. Be thankful to Him, and bless His name. For the Lord is good" (Psalms 100:4-5). We enter His gates with thanksgiving. A gate represents a new dimension or season of life. We can get out of any season where we feel stuck though a dramatic increase in our "thank yous" to God and people.

"Thank you" is a weapon with divine power to demolish strongholds of lack, hopelessness, and fear. It is also a main gateway into joy. Let's pull down negative strongholds in us and others through using this weapon like never before.

DAY 22
Why Do We Have to Fight For It?

"Little by little I will drive them out from before you, until you have increased, and you inherit the land"
(Exodus 23:30).

Sudden breakthrough, or little by little breakthrough, what do you choose?

The word "suddenly" appears in the Bible 87 times. This word helps us believe in immediate, unexpected breakthroughs in our own lives. It causes us to press into the power of God and the gifts of the Holy Spirit to bring amazing divine solutions to lives. It is a good thing.

The Children of Israel had many suddenlies. Some of them were:

- The parting of the Red Sea (Exodus 15)
- The walls of Jericho falling (Joshua 6)
- The sun stopping for Joshua (Joshua 10)

It is interesting, though, that the possession of their Promised Land was to be a slow process. As I consider this, my mind goes back to Numbers 13 when Moses sent out twelve spies to spy out the Promised Land. It was clear God was giving them this land (Numbers 13:2), so their assignment was to spy on the occupants of the land (the giants) and assess their strengths and weaknesses so they could get a battle plan to defeat them. Unfortunately, ten of the spies did not understand their task and came back with a negative conclusion about their ability to possess the land (which short-circuited God's will for their lives). On the other hand, the other two, Joshua and Caleb, believed in God's promise that they would possess the land.

As I think about this, I have a question. If God had already given them the land, then why did they need to fight to possess it? Shouldn't they have just gone in and taken it without any struggle?

You have probably heard that the struggle of the butterfly to get out of the cocoon is necessary for its wings to get strong enough to be able to fly. If the process is stopped, then the momentary freedom has long-lasting negative effects.

I once heard about a study of million-dollar lottery winners. After twenty years, 80% were back in the same economic state (or worse) as they were in before they won the lottery. This "suddenly" actually created more problems than it solved.

Similarly, we don't give the keys to our car to a five-year-old. They are not able to properly steward this "blessing".

"And no one puts new wine into old wineskins; or else the new wine bursts the wineskins, the wine is spilled, and the wineskins are ruined. But new wine must be put into new wineskins" (Mark 2:22). It is unwise to desire the "new wine" of dramatic increases in finances, favor, or fame without an equal commitment and desire for a stronger "wineskin" of integrity, identity beliefs, and generosity.

God has promised us victory, protection, health, abundance, miracles, answered prayers, and much more. It is our "Promised Land", but we have to fight to possess it. "Take up the sword of the Spirit, which is the word of God" (Ephesians 6:17). It is called a sword because we are to kill the lies fueling the giants we must overcome in our Promised Land. These giants are strongholds like pessimism, shame, disappointment, fear, offense, impulsiveness, victimhood, etc.

In the Old Testament, they displaced the giants in a lengthy process. "I will not drive them out from before you in one year, lest the land become desolate and the beasts of the field become too numerous for you. Little by little I will drive them out from before you, until you have increased, and you inherit the land" (Exodus 23:29-30). It is most often like this in our New Testament experience as well.

So why do we have to fight for our Promised Land? It is because of this truth: It is in the struggle that we build the character to be able to keep and increase the blessing given to us. It is in the process of displacing the enemy that we build the wineskin to attract the new wine we so desire.

"What does this have to do with joy?" you might ask. It has a lot to do with it because "character" is not just about actions, but more importantly about attitudes. Regular gladness at the level we are at is one of the main indicators we can be promoted into (and are able to handle) increase. A big part of the fight to possess our promises is the fight to keep our joy.

DAY 23
Why Are We Not Radically Joyful Now?

I have been very impacted by questions in the Bible. Here are some of my favorites:

- What are you doing here? (1 Kings 19:13)
- Who told you that? (Genesis 3:11)
- Can these bones live? (Ezekiel 37:3)
- Do you want to be made well? (John 5:6)
- What do you have? (2 Kings 4:2)

With these questions, God is not primarily wanting information, but He is setting the listener up for life-changing revelation.

In addition to the questions above, there are other questions God regularly asks me:

- What do you need to believe to have hope in this area?
- How much greatness is in the people in your life?
- Who do you think you are?
- Why are you not radically joyful now?

It is this last one, "Steve, why are you not radically joyful now?" that has impacted me much in recent years. I believe, as you join me in digging deep into our individual answers, we will be set up for massive growth for our lives.

It is clear from Scripture that God wants us to experience more than just a little joy. This is illustrated by the types of adjectives used describing joy. Here are a few examples of this:

- In His presence is fullness of joy (Psalm 16:11)
- Good tidings of great joy . . .for all the people (Luke 2:10)
- May the God of hope fill you with all joy (Romans 15:13)
- Consider it pure joy when you fall into various trials (James 1:2)
- These things I say to you so that your joy might be full (John 15:11; 1 John 1:14)
- Joy unspeakable and full of glory (1 Peter 1:8)

I have found few times in my life where it is convenient to walk in this kind of joy. There always seems to be a reason to delay it. Some of these reasons are:

- **Unworthiness** – I don't feel I deserve to walk in joy
- **Perfectionism** – I have to wait until things are perfect to be joyful
- **Non-eternity minded** – focused too much on the temporal rather than the eternal
- **Destination disease** – I am waiting for prayers to be answered or to have ideal circumstances to have joy
- **Relationships are not what I want them to be** – people I love are off course in their lives
- **Societal issues** – I have concerns about the direction of my country, etc.
- **Fear of letting go of guilt** – I am afraid if I become joyful I will stop working on important things I want to see changed in me
- **Judgements** – I disapprove of what the people around me are doing, and I don't want them to think they are ok
- **Passivity** – I just let life happen to me rather than walking in intentionality and passion
- **Fear of getting my hopes up again** – I don't want to experience disappointment again
- **Ungratefulness** – I focus on what I seemingly don't have rather than on what I do have
- **Negative comparison** – I see my faults more than my strengths

- **Victim mindset** – I believe someone else is responsible for my joy
- **Bad theology** – I believe God is not joyful

These are some of the main reasons (the "why") for my not possessing radical joy, and I have found when I face these root issues head on, I experience massive growth. The more we tackle the "why" keeping us from living in radical joy, the more we are setting ourself up to discover why joy is one-third of the kingdom (Romans 14:17). The kingdom will grow in and through us abundantly as we receive God's grace and truth for the belief systems blocking radical joy.

Years ago, I sensed the Lord say to me, "Steve, if you are not joyful now, the chances of you being joyful in the future are slim. Your lack of joy is not a circumstantial issue, but it is a YOU issue." At first, I did not like this and I thought, "Well, thanks, Lord. It always seems to come back to me. You are always trying to tell me how powerful I really am." I eventually understood what He was saying and started pursuing joy. It has been a surprising component of my spiritual growth plan.

I realize there are times where we will mourn or grieve. I do not want to imply we should not experience emotions like those, but we cannot make it a life-style as God's joy truly is our strength.

"Why are you not radically joyful now?" This question has been so good for me, and I believe it will catapult you too into maturity and great joy and freedom.

DAY 24
God Loves a Cheerful Decider

The following content is from my book, *Fully Convinced: The Art of Decision-Making*.

Here are three powerful quotes to lay the foundation for this devotional:

1. Cheerfulness is evidence we have attached faith to our decisions, responsibilities, assignments, and commitments.
2. Faithfulness is not just showing up, it is how you think when you show up.
3. Instead of waiting to do something great, attach great faith to what you are doing now and it will become great.

2 Corinthians 9 is a strong chapter about the attitudes and benefits of financial giving. It reveals incredible promises. We will:

- Reap generously if we sow generously
- Have all grace abounding to us
- Experience all-sufficiency
- Be enriched in every way to be generous in every way

Although there are many great promises in this chapter, let's focus on verse seven which speaks directly to my book's theme of being fully convinced.

"Each one must give as he has decided in his heart, not reluctantly or under compulsion, for God loves a cheerful giver" (2 Corinthians 9:7).

Let's break this verse down phrase by phrase:

- **Each one** – Each person is free to decide what they do and do not do. Although the Bible does give clear direction on many issues, there are also issues not clear-cut that we must decide on. In these cases, we must respect the decision-making and choices of others that are different from our own.
- **Must give as he has decided in his heart** – Again, we get to decide how much to give in finances, time, energy, and relationships. This is an incredible revelation as we move from a slave mentality to a son mentality. Slaves are always waiting for a command from God or from others to know what to do, but sons are given increasing authority to decide for themselves through good decision-making processes. Our good Father models excellent decision-making for us and then gives us room to try for ourselves. He enthusiastically celebrates when we choose well!
- **Not reluctantly or under compulsion** – If we have either one of these attitudes towards what we give ourselves to, they reveal one of two problems – we are either doing the wrong thing or we are doing the right thing with the wrong beliefs. "Therefore let us leave the elementary doctrine of Christ and go on to maturity, not laying again a foundation of repentance from dead works and of faith toward God" (Hebrews 6:1). A dead work is Christian "obedience" done consistently in a reluctant manner or under compulsion (not being done in faith). Repentance from this is one of the elementary doctrines of Christ.
- **For God loves a cheerful giver** – The Greek word for cheerful is "hilaros", from which we get our word hilarious (boisterous merriment). Cheerfulness is evidence we have attached faith to our decisions. God loves a cheerful giver because that kind of person gives from their heart in faith. As they give, they think, "This is exciting. I have decided to do this. This is going to have a huge positive impact on me and others." Note: many churches

do offering declaration readings before the offering to stir up this cheerfulness.

Again, the principles of 2 Corinthians 9:7 are applicable far beyond finances, and we can rightly conclude that God loves a cheerful decider. A chronic lack of cheerfulness in our disciplines, decisions, schedules, commitments, or responsibilities is almost always a sign we have decided out of obligation instead of faith. When we recognize we are not cheerful concerning our choices, then it is a sign we have a decision to make. Here is how to do this:

1. **Clarify your options and decide what you are to do** – This is the key to living in faith concerning what we have decided to do. One option is most certainly to continue doing what we are doing without cheerfulness, but that is not a good option. What we need to do is get a good process for decision-making and then decide what to do. My book, *Fully Convinced: The Art of Decision-Making*, goes into great detail on how to have this good process.

2. **Speak life over your commitments** – "My meetings today are going to be powerful," or "God is going to show up in my family tonight when I get home," or "This coffee meeting with my friend will cause a breakthrough for both of us." One of the greatest ways to attach faith to what we are doing, and who we are, is to make faith declarations.

3. **Press into your beliefs until cheerfulness manifests consistently regarding the choices you have made** – This may take a while, but the journey is incredible as we go deeper in defeating the lies that create a lack of cheerfulness in giving our time, finances, passion, and energy.

God loves a cheerful decider because it is a significant sign of spiritual maturity. Our Heavenly Father, as with any parent, loves it when His kids move from indecision to confidence in what they decide to do. 2 Corinthians 9:7 is a great verse to meditate on for the one who desires to be fully convinced (and to increase their joy).

DAY 25
Reflection, Activation, and Advanced Research on Joy

Reflection questions:

1. Which of the four devotionals in this section spoke to you the most and why?
2. What do you believe God is saying to you personally through these devotionals?
3. What is one area where you realize you are not a cheerful decider that you can apply the principles of day 24?
4. Who can you encourage today through a voice message, text, phone call, email, or in some other way? Remember that encouraging others is a great way to increase your own joy.

Advanced Research on Joy by Dr. Pieter Lagaay
The Connection Between Joy and Success

The idea that you can't have joy without having success first simply isn't true. This truth was written on a piece of paper by Albert Einstein and sold for 1.3 million dollars, *"A calm and modest life brings more happiness than the pursuit of success combined with constant restlessness."* In 2005 a group of psychologists aimed to prove that joyful people are likely to acquire favorable life circumstances. The study was published in the *Psychological Bulletin* and demonstrated that people who experience a preponderance of joy tend to be successful and accomplished across multiple life domains.

In this study, joyful employees high in dispositional joy received more favorable evaluations from supervisors. In another study sampling three Midwestern organizations, managers of high joy employees gave them higher evaluations for work quality, productivity, dependability, and creativity. In 1999, these results were duplicated in another study showing that joyful people receive higher ratings from supervisors.

In 2000, a conclusory study was published finding that work performance appeared more strongly predicted by joy than by job satisfaction. This study demonstrated that job performance, as judged by supervisors, was significantly correlated with joyful employees, but uncorrelated with measures of job satisfaction. This means that joyfulness was not related to job satisfaction.

Joyful employees are also less likely to experience burnout and more likely to achieve promotions and attain managerial positions. The previous 2005 study concluded that joyful employees were more likely to experience increases in their income. The results show that people who experience joy more frequently also experience later financial prosperity.

Activation

Believing that joy will lead to success means that we also need to find joy in our work. What we do for work, whether we are an employee, parent, student, or volunteer is not as important as remembering who we are with when we are working. "You will show me the path of life; In Your presence is fullness of joy; At Your right hand are pleasures forevermore" (Psalms 16:11). This promise is both a promise that God will show us the path and a declaration by David that when we are in God's presence we will encounter joy.

1. Take 3-5 minutes to pray and ask God what part of His nature gives you the greatest sense of His presence? Let your spirit wander and draw as close as possible to His spirit while staying focused on God's presence.
2. Whatever God revealed to you, hold on to that encounter for the rest of the day. Throughout your day while you are working, parenting, volunteering or whatever you're doing, just keep thanking God for being in His presence.

DAY 26
When You Feel Like Giving Up

To quit means to stop, cease, or discontinue doing something. It is giving up, resigning, letting go, or relinquishing. Good parents teach their children to not get into the habit of starting things and then quitting when the going gets tough. Even so, we have all felt like quitting concerning specific things in our lives (whether small or big commitments or dreams).

There certainly are things we should quit, such as a bad habit, a toxic relationship, a self-limiting belief, or an assignment bearing no fruit. We are wise to decide to stop putting our energy into destructive or non-fruit-producing investments such as these. The focus of this devotional, however, is not about what we ought to leave behind, it's about things we should not quit.

When we feel like quitting, Galatians 6:9 is a good verse to meditate on, "And let us not grow weary while doing good, for in due season we shall reap if we do not lose heart." This is a tremendous verse of promise. **From it, we learn:**

- **There is something good for us to do** – These are investments of love, prayer, faith, and obedience we are called to give.
- **We can grow weary and lose heart** – When we focus mainly on the results of our investments, instead of focusing on attaching faith to what we are doing, we will increasingly become weary and lose heart.

- **There is a due season coming** – Just as in farming, there are specific seasons for the planting, watering, and harvesting cycle. It is impossible to plant and water, and not have a harvest.
- **We shall reap** – Earlier in chapter six, Paul wrote, "For whatever a man sows, that he will also reap" (Galatians 6:7). What good things have you been sowing? Love? Finances? Prayer? Encouragement? Freedom? Healing? As you consider these, release your faith right now that a harvest is coming for what you have sown.

Here are some things I do when I feel like quitting.

- Watch videos of boxers who looked like they were going to lose, but eventually won (the Rocky movie series often helps me to "stay in the game")
- Get rest
- Have fun and laugh
- Hang out with people who inspire and understand you
- Get a strategy and plan concerning the things causing discouragement

"For a righteous man may fall seven times and rise again" (Proverbs 24:16). You are an overcomer. This feeling of wanting to quit will pass.

In conclusion, here are some great quotes to inspire you to not quit today:

- "I think I can. I think I can. I think I can. I know I can." – Watty Piper, The Little Engine That Could
- "Our greatest weakness lies in giving up. The most certain way to succeed is always to try just one more time." – Thomas Edison
- "Survival can be summed up in three words — never give up. That's the heart of it, really. Just keep trying." – Bear Grylls
- "It's not that I'm so smart, it's just that I stay with problems longer." – Albert Einstein
- "Life is like riding a bicycle. To keep your balance, you must keep moving." – Albert Einstein
- "If opportunity doesn't knock, build a door." – Milton Berle

- "Never give up, for that is just the place and time that the tide will turn." – Harriet Beecher Stowe
- "If you're going through hell, keep going." – Winston Churchill
- "Success is moving from failure to failure without losing enthusiasm." – Winston Churchill
- "You do what you can for as long as you can, and when you finally can't, you do the next best thing. You back up but you don't give up." – Chuck Yeager
- "You are never too old to set another goal or to dream a new dream." – C.S. Lewis
- "When you feel like quitting, think about why you started." – Anonymous
- "Failure is success in progress."- Albert Einstein
- "I have not failed, I have just found 10,000 ways that won't work." – Thomas Edison
- "It always seems impossible until it's done." – Nelson Mandela
- "Successful men and women keep moving. They make mistakes, but they don't quit." – Conrad Hilton
- "By perseverance, the snail reached the ark." – Charles Spurgeon

Perseverance, resilience, and adaptability are qualities that high-level joy carriers keep growing in.

DAY 27
Living in Childlike Joy & Wonder

My definition of joy is this: **The childlike wonder and excitement of working with God instead of working for God.** This attitude and philosophy is in keeping with what Jesus said in Matthew 18:3. "Unless you are converted and become as little children, you will not enter the kingdom . . ."

It is impossible under a religious mindset to have true joy because religion only becomes joyful with perfection, while family celebrates and becomes joyful with progress. Performance-based living blocks the cheerful heart, as do negative mindsets (such as slave, servant, and orphan mindsets), but as we embrace the heart of a son or daughter to our Father, we also embrace walking in greater joy.

Wherever you find real hope, you will find "all joy" too. "Now may the God of hope fill you with all joy and peace in believing" (Romans 15:13). Increasing hope and joy is the fruit of having good beliefs. Many affirm good doctrines but are plagued by bad beliefs (believing lies about God, themselves, others and circumstances).

Let's look at four components concerning my definition of joy:

1. **Childlike wonder** – Little children see the world with fresh eyes. My grandchildren re-energize my excitement for life through their excitement for things I have grown too familiar with. I believe wonder is like a muscle we can strengthen in our lives.

Bill Johnson, senior leader at Bethel Church in Redding, CA, has built a culture where we passionately celebrate testimonies people share of what God has done. We applaud. We stand. We shout because He is "WONDERful". We can develop this in other areas as well.

2. **Adventure** – "Delight yourself in the Lord, and He will give you the desires of your heart" (Psalm 37:4). Here is the Backlund expanded version of this verse:

    "Enjoy yourself in the Lord. Relish in His goodness. Revel in the adventure of walking with Him. Savor every moment with Him. Delight in His unconditional love. Get over condemnation, unworthiness, introspection and false humility; and become like a little child in a candy shop with Him."

3. **Excitement** – Excitement is a feeling of great enthusiasm and eagerness. It is illustrated by children anticipating Christmas morning. It is the opposite of boredom. It is an attitude we can develop by attaching faith to who we are and what we are doing. Sports teams understand they not only need skills and a good plan, but they also need inner fire (excitement for the opportunity ahead of them). I remember years ago when I felt like the Lord said to me, "Steve, always act more enthusiastic than you feel." Enthusiasm and excitement are "muscles" we can develop. They are what allow us to be thermostats and not thermometers, in our homes, churches, at work, and everywhere else. Joy people frequently say, "This is so exciting!"

4. **Working With God** – God partners with our ideas, our thoughts, our hopes, our prophetic acts, our words, and our actions. "Steve, give Me something to work with" was a clear word He spoke to me years ago. For example, Jesus did not create wine out of thin air in John 2. He said, "Give me those pots. Put some water in them." He needed something to partner with. When we understand this, and when we understand His heart to have fun with us, then we develop a whole new mindset of doing life and ministry with Him.

5. **Not Working For God** – How do we know if we are working for God, instead of working with God? Some of the signs are perfectionism, chronic fear of punishment, being overly obedience-focused, not getting hope every time we read the Bible, and letting apparent failure in an area of our lives create an identity for us.

Activation

Joy is the childlike wonder and excitement of working with God instead of working for God. Why don't you meditate on each of these words again and imagine what it would look like for you to live this out?

DAY 28
5 Things to Let Go of Now

In India, farmers had problems with monkeys stealing their crops so they designed a trap to catch them. They would tie a coconut to the side of a tree, cut a small hole inside the coconut and place a banana within the hole. When a monkey would smell the banana, it would stick its hand inside the hole to grab the fruit, but the hole was too small to let the monkey get both its hand and the banana out. Unwilling to let go of the banana, the monkey would stay in the same spot until it got caught.

In the same way, we can sometimes refuse to let go of things that are not good for us and that restrict our joy.

Here are five things that are not worth holding onto:

1. **The need to always be right** – We can be right with the facts but completely wrong in our attitude or in our timing. The Pharisees were technically right in bringing the woman caught in adultery to Jesus, but they were totally wrong in the heart behind the action. Here are some habits that can help us let go of our need to be right:
    *   Holding our tongue – "Even a fool is thought wise when he holds his tongue" (Proverbs 17:28)
    *   Seeking to understand before seeking to be understood – this will soften your heart toward others
    *   Choosing our battles wisely – don't major in minor issues

2. **Being isolated** – Elijah was alone in a cave in 1 Kings 19. Isolation tends to cause us to be delusional in our thinking as it did with Elijah. It also increases the likelihood of developing harmful habits and addictions. 1 John 1:7 gives us the motivation to come out of the cave of isolation. It says, "But if we walk in the light as He is in the light, we have fellowship with one another, and the blood of Jesus Christ His Son cleanses us from all sin." As we spiritually connect with others, it will catalyze victory for us. Here are some ideas for how to let go of isolation:
   - Join others in a cause – move forward by partnering with others to make a difference
   - Be a part of a growth group – commit to a group of believers and regularly connect with a small group
   - Get help as needed – there is no shame in needing to see a counselor to address emotional and lifestyle problems

3. **The need to keep things the way they are** – Again, the Pharisees could not embrace Jesus and the new season he represented because they were more focused on preserving the past. The fear of change blocks many from being a part of what God is doing now. Here are some ways to increase the likelihood of embracing the good, new things in life:
   - Be willing to let others become more prominent than you – John the Baptist did this with Jesus, but King Saul refused to do so concerning David. The first was exalted and the second lost his kingdom.
   - Regularly ask the Holy Spirit this question: What are the new things You are doing? – Certainly, we don't want to waver in commitments we have already made or in areas the Lord has spoken to us about previously, but we also do not want to get stuck in the past and miss the new thing God is doing.
   - Realize there will be times in our lives when we will need to do things that seem illogical to our human reasoning – If we only make decisions based on what might increase our popularity, finances, safety, or vocational success, we will miss some very important life-launching opportunities. We are not called to be realistic, we are called to be supernatural.

4. **Wrong definitions of success** – Success is not a goal to be attained, but it is a state of being. If we need anything outward to cause us to believe we are successful, then we really aren't successful. Great leaders become successful in their beliefs before they become successful externally. Here are some keys to help you let go of wrong definitions of success:

   - Deal with unsuspecting sources of shame – This can be shame about our appearance, possessions, family situation, vocation, spiritual gifts, or something else.
   - Value inner success more than outer success – what is happening in us is ultimately more important than what is happening through us or around us.
   - Consume the Book of Proverbs – there are thirty-one chapters (one for each day of the month)

5. **Preconceived ideas of what God is going to do** – In 2 Kings 5, Namaan was angry because Elisha did not do what he expected in prescribing healing for his leprosy. Also, the Pharisees (and pretty much everyone else) missed the Messiah (Jesus) because He did not come as expected. Here are some practices to help us let go of the preconceived idea mindset:

   - Adding hope to our faith – Hope is an overall optimistic attitude about the future based on the goodness and promises of God. If our ability to thrive in life is dependent on specific prayers being answered, then we will not experience the abundant life Jesus promised.
   - Studying biblical examples of supernatural, creative solutions – As we study the different kinds of miracles in the Bible, we will be stirred to expect God to come in creative, different ways.
   - Being objective about our first reaction to new revelation and new ways people seem to be getting breakthrough, especially if the reaction is negative – Many times I have been uncomfortable and troubled by something I have heard or seen in church, but later, I found out it had solid scriptural support.

Let's not "monkey around" by holding on to things that restrict our victory, influence, and joy. Instead, let's ask God to help us let go of the things we need to let go of.

DAY 29
"I Have To" Vs. "I Get To"

"Then said I (Jeremiah): 'Ah, Lord God! Behold, I cannot speak, for I am a youth.' **But the Lord said to me: 'Do not say, 'I *am* a youth'"**

(Jeremiah 1:6-7).

There are many times I have sensed God saying to me, "Steve, do not say THAT." Here are some examples of things I am not to say:

- **"I cannot afford it"** – this most likely results from a victim mindset. It is better to say, "I don't want to spend the money on that right now."
- **"I don't have enough time to do that"** – this is another statement reflecting we do not believe we are powerful. An alternative is to say, "This is not a priority for me right now" or "I already have a commitment for that time."
- **"I am not good at"** – the more we hear ourselves agreeing with our past experience, the more we will believe something that will unnecessarily limit our potential.
- **"is hard for me"** – those who repeatedly confess something is hard will create unnecessary difficulty for themselves.
- **"I have to"** – this will be the main focus of this teaching.

Why do we say what we say? In my mentoring of people, one of the most important things I focus on is helping people become students of their own words. If we can understand the beliefs behind the words we speak, then we are being set up for massive transformation.

"For we all stumble in many things. If anyone does not stumble in word, he *is* a perfect man, able also to bridle the whole body" (James 3:2). James says if we control our words, we can control our lives.

"Out of the abundance of the heart, the mouth speaks" (Matthew 12:34). Our words do indeed shine a light on what we believe. They will reveal what we believe about ourselves, others, the future, our nation, and whether we believe our prayers are being answered.

Let me be clear, I am not saying we should not share with others about the struggles we might be having, but we want to avoid making concluding statements about our identity, our future, and about other people from those struggles.

Now, let's talk about "I have to" vs. "I get to." The words "I have to" reflect a lack of attaching faith to what we are doing. They reveal an, "I am doing this out of duty or obligation" mindset rather than a mindset of significance and unlimited potential.

Faithfulness is not just showing up to do something, but it is showing up full of faith (faithful). Faithfulness is more of a mindset than outward action. Certainly, we need to learn to show up when we don't feel like showing up, but the Kingdom of God is not moved forward by good conduct; it is moved forward by good beliefs (Galatians 3:1-5). What I believe is ultimately more important than what I do, and if I have good beliefs, I will see transformation in my actions and influence (Romans 12:2).

"I get to." This simple switch from "I have to" will be catalytic for our growth. To consistently speak this out, we will be overcoming:

- Doubt and double-mindedness concerning our commitments
- Dead, lifeless works
- Passivity

- Unbelief concerning the significance of what we are doing
- Spiritual tiredness
- Beliefs that our words are not powerful

I bless you in eliminating "I have to . . ." from your life and replacing it with "I get to . . ." It changes things more than you might think, and it will help increase your joy.

DAY 30
Reflection, Activation, and Advanced Research on Joy

Reflection questions:

1. Which of the four devotionals in this section spoke to you the most and why?
2. What do you believe God is saying to you personally through these devotionals?
3. Who can you encourage today through a voice message, text, phone call, email, or in some other way? Remember that encouraging others is a great way to increase your own joy.

Advanced Research on Joy by Dr. Pieter Lagaay
Joy at Work Heals Others

That feeling of joylessness while at work is a mindset that much of the world carries like a badge of honor. If I persevere despite joylessness then I can celebrate the sacrifices I am making for my family and myself. This martyr mentality is a stronghold and a major cause of burnout in vocational careers and impeding the prosperity of our souls.

Understanding what joy is, and how it differs from happiness is important because happiness deceives us into believing we are filled with joy. David Brooks (NY Times columnist) is quoted as saying "Happiness involves a victory of self. Joy involves the transcendence of self. Happiness comes from accomplishments. True joy is the present that life gives you as you give away your gifts." (NY Times 2019).

To understand the impact of joylessness in the workplace, the medical field is a great example. In 2018, physicians had the highest suicide rate and one-third of physicians suffered from clinical depression. In a field where physicians take an oath that explicitly says "May I always act so as to preserve the finest traditions of my calling and may I long to experience the **joy** of healing those who seek my help", it is rarely a place of joy.

The importance of joy is not only specific to the medical workplace. God tells us just how vital it is to all of us! Proverbs 17:22 tells us, "A merry heart is good medicine, but a crushed spirit dries up the bones." The word heart in Hebrew means inner man or soul, while the word medicine means a cure. The revelation Solomon received almost 3,000 years ago provides the answer to curing our souls. It is joy!

Paul later tells us in Romans 15:13 that since we already believe Jesus is our Lord and Saviour, we are also already filled with joy! "May the God of hope fill you with all joy and peace in believing, so that by the power of the Holy Spirit you may abound in hope." So the good news is we already have joy, but we need to be fully convinced of this fact. Just as physicians long to experience the joy of healing, our souls long to experience joy. No matter what job you have, joy is good medicine to heal yourself and others.

Activation

Find a situation at work (or school, church, etc.) that you and others find little joy in. Invite a coworker to make positive declarations with you.

Start by making positive declarations specifically over the other person. These declarations should be in direct opposition to what you and your coworker are believing about the situation causing your lack of joy.

Make ridiculous positive declarations that cause each of you to laugh about the situation you find little joy in.

Give your coworker a high five and say "This is going to be the best (fill in the blank) ever!"

If you do not have a co-worker to partner with, then you can:

- Make personal declarations (yes, even ridiculous ones) over the situation.
- Be the most encouraging, cheerful, and thankful person imaginable in the situation.

DAY 31
Cancel the Cancel Culture

A cancel culture greatly decreases joy in our lives and our relationships.

Cancel culture is a modern form of ostracism (shunning) in which someone is thrust out of social or professional circles – whether it be online, on social media, or in person. Those who are subject to this ostracism are said to have been "canceled".

Cancel culture is a non-biblical response to the perceived faults and failures of others. It is the opposite of the heart of Galatians 6:1. "Brethren, if a man is overtaken in any trespass, you who *are* spiritual restore such a one in a spirit of gentleness, considering yourself lest you also be tempted." We may not agree with people's behavior, but we are called to have a heart of restoration, not a heart to cancel.

Jesus told the Scribes and Pharisees, "He who is without sin among you, let him throw a stone at her first" (John 8:7). Everyone has something in their life that they would not want written about on the front page of a newspaper. Even many of our favorite Bible characters did things that were embarrassing, scandalous, or just plain wrong. Peter is one of these.

"Now Simon Peter stood and warmed himself. Therefore they said to him, 'You are not also *one* of His disciples, are you?' **He denied *it* and said, 'I am not!'** One of the servants of the high priest, a relative *of him* whose ear Peter cut off, said, 'Did I not see you in the garden with

Him?' Peter then denied again; and immediately a rooster crowed" (John 18:26-27).

The Bible is not afraid of letting us see the faults of the men and women God used (i.e. David's adultery and murder, Jacob's dishonesty, Jonah's running from God and his negative attitude, etc.). Part of the reason for this is so we won't deify people because If we do this, we will believe we are too shameful to be used by God, and we will actually cancel ourselves (which is the beginning step to canceling others).

How we respond to the failures of others is a big indicator of how spiritual we are and how much God can trust us with people. "You who *are* spiritual restore such a one (the one overtaken in a trespass) in a spirit of gentleness." We know we are spiritual and have a heart for restoration if:

- We hurt for and pray for major ministry leaders who have a moral or other failure.
- We realize we too could do something very stupid if not for the grace of God in our lives.
- We first give the benefit of doubt that people think they are doing the right thing.
- We first seek to understand before we seek to be understood.
- We first try to take the telephone pole out of our eye before trying to take the speck out of someone else's eye (Matthew 7:1-5).

In Luke 15, the prodigal son was not canceled by his father. "And he arose and came to his father. But when he was still a great way off, his father saw him and had compassion, and ran and fell on his neck and kissed him" (Luke 15:20). The father blessed his son and threw a party for him. In contrast, the older brother of the prodigal canceled him. "But he was angry and would not go in (to celebrate with his brother)" (vs 28).

God's plan for our lives is to move us from an elder brother mindset to a father mindset. The default of an elder brother mindset is to first see what is wrong with a person or place, but the default of a father mindset is to first see what is right with a person or place. Yes, we do not want to be gullible concerning people, but if we are going to err on any side, it would be better to believe in people too much.

"Brethren, if a man is overtaken in any trespass . . ." When people fail around us, it is a great opportunity to bring healing and deepen our heart connection. There have been seasons in my ministry where sins were being exposed and lives were seemingly falling apart. I asked the Lord, "Does this mean I am not a good leader?" In response, I heard this, "Steve, these things have been in their lives for a long time, but I have hidden them because they were not in a place where they could be restored in a spirit of gentleness. These problems manifesting are actually a sign you are a good leader."

So, let's cancel the cancel culture concerning ourselves and others. Let's truly be spiritual and embrace our assignment to be those who have a heart to restore and not cut off and shame those who have done wrong. It will bring joy to others and to ourselves.

DAY 32
Celebrating Progress

Just as we celebrate a toddler who is making progress in learning to walk, we are to celebrate our own progress. With toddlers, we focus on what they are doing well instead of dwelling on what they are not doing well. The same strategy will work for us as we learn to step into new areas of growth in our lives. Our gifts will get stronger as we praise our own accomplishments.

Even though most would agree with the above, it is not common to have this attitude toward ourselves. Here are three reasons for this:

1. **The belief that guilt and condemnation are necessary motivation tools** – Many believe that if we don't use guilt and condemnation to motivate ourselves, we might think we are okay and stop working on things.

2. **The fear that celebration will only lead to pride** – Pride doesn't mean that we think we're great; it means we think we are greater than other people. There is greatness in each one of us that is needed to make the world a better place.

3. **The belief that God is not celebrating what we are doing, so why should we?** – God is celebrating that Jesus died and took our place. Just as God celebrated Jesus on earth, He is celebrating those who believe in Jesus right now. (Note: If you doubt this, then I suggest feasting on teaching about the

finished works of Jesus and about our new spiritual birth when we become born again. Joseph Prince has great material for this.)

Here are five compelling reasons for celebrating progress in your life:

1. **It opens our eyes to where grace is manifesting in us** – Paul states in Philippians 1:6 that he "is confident that He who has begun a good work in (us) will complete it." We are not to have faith in our ability to perform well, but we are to have faith in God's ability to complete what He started in and through us. It is a process, and celebrating progress reminds us of this.

2. **It helps silence the accuser's voice of condemnation toward us** – One of the most used weapons of the enemy is to tell us who we are not. As we celebrate progress in who we are and what we are growing in, we take a major step in silencing these accusations.

3. **It creates momentum for us and gives us something to build on for the future** – When David approached Goliath, he rehearsed his victories and celebrated his progress ("I've killed a lion and a bear"), and through this, he gained momentum in his life for the battle that he was facing at that moment.

4. **It increases the joy of the Lord in our lives** – When we see the joy of a family applauding a toddler learning to walk, we discern that an atmosphere of joy and gladness is vital for people to grow into their potential. The Bible says "The joy of the Lord is your strength" (Nehemiah 8:10). We all desire more joy, and celebrating our progress is one more tool to increase our gladness. Try rejoicing over yourself as much as a family would over their toddler.

5. **It will increase our celebration of others** – "Love your neighbor as you love yourself" (Matthew 29:39). How we treat ourselves will be how we treat others. If we celebrate our own progress,

we will celebrate the progress of others and then function in one of the most needed gifts – encouragement.

Here are examples of where I have celebrated my progress:

- In my hope and joy journey
- In my eating habits
- In keeping heart connection with people
- In resting and relaxing more

None of these are where I want them to ultimately be. There are times when I "fall" as I am trying to walk consistently in them, but I recognize I am doing better. Woo hoo! I celebrate myself.

Activation

Let me ask you this. What areas are you improving? Take a few moments to identify one or more places in your life where you can celebrate yourself. You really do have more successes than failures! You might not believe it, but if you consider areas where you have overcome and refused to give up, celebrating your progress will be easy!

DAY 33
Positive Thinking Vs. Biblical Optimism

"Let us hold fast the confession of our hope without wavering, for He who promised is faithful."
(Hebrews 10:23)

I frequently say, "I am not a proponent of positive thinking but of biblical optimism." Certainly, positive thinking has its benefits, but we cannot simply have a "mind over matter" approach in our thinking. Our positivity needs to be anchored to something eternal and unchanging.

Positive thinking means we approach unpleasantness in a more positive and productive way. We think the best is going to happen, not the worst.

As early as the first century, writers like Epictetus were saying, "The thing that upsets people is not so much what happens, but what they think about what happens."

Norman Vincent Peale, a Methodist minister, wrote the best-selling book, *The Power of Positive Thinking* in 1952, and over fifteen million copies have been sold to date. I have read the book, and it greatly impacted my thinking and theology by giving me biblical insights into the power of beliefs.

When I say, "I am not a proponent of positive thinking", I am saying that positive thinking apart from a committed relationship to Jesus lacks the most important ingredient for real, lasting positivity. If we try to live Romans 12:2 ("be transformed by the renewing of your mind"), without first establishing Romans 12:1 ("present your bodies as a living sacrifice"), then our mind renewal (positive thinking) will have deception in it.

With that said, I believe many believers would greatly benefit from listening to biblically-based "positive thinking" teachers and preachers. This should not be the only food in our spiritual diet, but without it, we will most likely be living joylessly and pessimistically, feeling unworthy, and falling far short of our potential.

My favorite definition of hope is this: Hope is the belief that the future will be better than the present, and I have the power to help make it so. Hope certainly is a positive perspective on life and the future. Here are two other great definitions of hope:

- Hope is an overall optimistic attitude about the future based on the goodness and promises of God.
- Hope is the confident, joyful expectancy that good is coming.

The more truth we believe, the more optimistic we will be; but the more lies we believe, the more pessimistic we will be. "Now may the God of hope fill you with all joy and peace in believing, that you may abound in hope by the power of the Holy Spirit." (Romans 15:13)

So how do we get biblical optimism into our lives? We get it through meditating on and speaking the promises of God. Our biblical optimism will grow massively as we believe promises like these:

- **God is faithful** – The more we believe He is faithful, the more optimistic our thoughts and words will be. "Let us hold fast the confession of our hope without wavering, for He who promised is faithful." (Hebrews 10:23)
- **Our prayers are working and changing things** – Much of our confident, joyful expectancy comes from believing our prayers are powerful and effective. "Now this is the confidence that we have in Him, that if we ask anything according to His will, He

hears us. And if we know that He hears us, whatever we ask, we know that we have the petitions that we have asked of Him." (1 John 5:14-15)

- **All things are working for our good** – If it is not good yet, He is not done working. "And we know that all things work together for good to those who love God, to those who are called according to His purpose." (Romans 8:28)
- **He is currently completing what He has started in us and around us** – My faith is not in me, but in His ability to bring things to a positive completion. "Being confident of this very thing, that He who began a good work in you will complete it until the day of Jesus Christ." (Philippians 1:6)

There are many more promises we could mention that will create a supernatural experience for our future. 2 Peter 1:4 tells us this: "By which have been given to us exceedingly great and precious promises, that through these you may be partakers of the divine nature." Part of participating in the divine is to have hope (optimism for the future). Truly, our futures are as bright as the promises of God. And, of course, our optimism will go off the charts as we gain greater revelation that we have eternal life through Jesus, and we will be with our Lord forever and ever after this life ends.

Yes, I am a biblical optimist. It is absolutely a positive, joyful way of thinking that is connected to the unchanging love and faithfulness of God. Let's be powerful carriers of hope to those around us like never before.

DAY 34
Defeating the Giant of Negative Comparison

Have you ever felt insecure because someone could do something better than you? Have you ever been tempted to think negatively about someone who was celebrated more than you? Well, if you have (and who hasn't?), then this devotional is for you. We will learn from the life of Saul about what not to do, and then get revelation of the importance of celebrating the success of others (and the importance of attaching faith to the skill level we have now).

Saul was Israel's first king, He was a very skilled man, but he battled the same lies we do. Ultimately, his inability to defeat these lies created an insecurity and emotional immaturity which led to his downfall. This was made evident when he became aware of how people were talking about a young man named David.

"So the women sang as they danced, and said: '**Saul has slain his thousands, and David his ten thousands**.' Then Saul was very angry, and the saying displeased him; and he said, 'They have ascribed to David ten thousands, and to me they have ascribed *only* thousands. Now what more can he have but the kingdom?' So Saul eyed David from that day forward" (1 Samuel 18:7-9).

Here are some truths that stand out to me from this passage:

- Saul was a mighty warrior and worthy of praise.
- Even so, David was a greater warrior than him.
- There will always be people who do what we do much better than us.
- How we respond to this will be one of the indicators of how much God can trust us in the future with favor and increase.
- If we allow someone who "kills their ten thousands" to stop us from valuing our "thousands,' we will be unwise and greatly limit our influence.
- Just as it was with King Saul, there will also be many people who wish they could be as effective as us.

We can certainly relate to Saul's experience:

- We may not be as compassionate and selfless as Mother Theresa, but our love still makes a difference.
- We may not be as great a businessperson as Bill Gates, but our business still provides jobs and helps many.
- We may not be as great at bringing miracles as Benny Hinn, but our healing anointing has canceled sickness and brought health to many lives.
- We may not be as strong of a worship leader as Brian Johnson or Kim Walker Smith, but our worship still brings honor to the Lord and moves His heart.
- We may not be as strong of a preacher as TD Jakes, but our sharing the Gospel rescues the lost and brings people into the glorious kingdom.
- We may not be able to experience the realm of the Spirit as much as Wendy Backlund, but the level we are at creates encounters for others.
- We may not have as many online followers as John Maxwell, but our material is still bringing breakthroughs to lives, families, and nations.

In today's social media age, we can regularly see people who are seemingly having "ten thousands" experiences in family, possessions, influence, beauty, and happiness while we feel we are having a "thousands" experience in these.

We have seen through the life of Saul how not to respond to our shortcomings. Let's now consider someone who responded differently – David. He could have responded out of the same insecurity. He was:

- a child
- a shepherd
- an unchosen son when his father presented his sons to Samuel
- uneducated
- untrained in the way of Kings
- untrained as a soldier
- rejected
- despised by his brothers

David didn't compare his gifts to others – he just offered them all to God and found out God can do a lot with whatever we freely offer Him.

David knew that negative comparison is not an effective growth tool. Instead, it only highlights where we are not measuring up to what others are doing. But when we learn to celebrate the big wins in others' lives while also valuing what we bring to the table, we will see our influence and skills continue to grow. God has not called us to be someone else, He has called us to be ourselves. And, you walking in the fullness of who God made you is the most impactful you could ever be.

Yes, let's keep growing and becoming more skilled, but let's also realize there will always be people to celebrate with greater ability than us who will give us great opportunities to reject insecurity and jealousy. As we defeat the giant of negative comparison, we will certainly become more joyful and more influential. Saul missed his opportunity; let's not miss ours.

DAY 35
Reflection, Activation, and Advanced Research on Joy

Reflection questions:

1. Which of the four devotionals in this section spoke to you the most and why?
2. What do you believe God is saying to you personally through these devotionals?
3. Who can you encourage today through a voice message, text, phone call, email, or in some other way? Remember that encouraging others is a great way to increase your own joy.

Advanced Research on Joy by Dr. Pieter Lagaay Psychoneuroimmunology – Overcoming the "Worried Sick"

Advanced Research on Joy by Dr. Pieter Lagaay Psychoneuroimmunology- Overcoming the "Worried Sick" Attitude Psychoneuroimmunology (PNI) studies how subjective moods connect with the vastly complex physiology of the nervous and immune systems. **Simply put, PNI aims to answer the question of, "Does joy strengthen the immune system?"** Several studies strongly suggest that the answer to this question is yes, which helps explain the expression of being "worried sick".

It is well understood that isolation, depression and generalized joylessness decrease the production of various cells that are critical in fighting off all sorts of infections. However, more recently, several studies have also demonstrated the opposite. Joy increases the cellular production of our immune system. One study demonstrated that the production of white blood cells (the main type of cells that fight off infection) increased when people specifically focused on being joyful.

Using joy to increase your immune system also depends on the type of joy you have. Joy that is obtained through a temporal experience like having an amazing meal has a different effect on our immune system than a deeper joy which persists beyond the time of an experience and positively creates identity in oneself. Researchers found people with a positive identity of self that was meaning-based or purpose-based had a greater production of immune system cells than people who had joy from a temporal experience.

Obtaining a deeper joy to boost our immune system begins with believing in a positive identity about ourselves. This starts with knowing and believing who we are in Christ. Prophecy is a practical tool that God has given us to strengthen our identity and enable us to experience a deeper joy because it is rooted in encouragement, edification, and exhortation (1 Corinthians 14:3). Perhaps this is one of the reasons Paul says, "Pursue love and desire spiritual gifts, but especially that you may prophesy." (1 Corinthians 14:1). Albeit, it is wonderful to receive prophetic words from others to experience deeper joy, it is vital to prophesy over ourselves and believe the positive identity God is speaking over us. The deeper joy which results from prophecy increases the production and efficiency of our immune system because it positively builds up our identity, which is not temporal. We can find eternal joy if we believe the prophetic words we speak over ourselves. When we continuously renew our minds with God's word about who we are in Christ, we increase our body's immune system to fight infections and sickness.

Activation

1. Find a verse or passage in scripture that encourages, edifies and exhorts you. It should positively speak into your identity.
2. Start your day by speaking out this verse or passage. Then throughout the day, if you feel discouraged or joyless, speak out this verse or passage, and end your day by thanking God for His promises over you.

DAY 36
This is the Real Problem

In the 90's, when my wife, Wendy, and I were learning about hope, we heard this great quote by Francis Frangipane: "Any area of your life that doesn't glisten with hope is under the influence of a lie and that area is a stronghold of the devil in your life." Romans 15:13 confirms that quote: "Now may the God of hope fill you with **all joy** and peace in believing that you may abound in hope by the power of the Holy Spirit." Increasing hope is the evidence that the renewal of the mind is happening with truth instead of lies. Decreasing hope is the evidence we are renewing our minds with lies instead of truth.

As we were processing these revelations about hope, we felt like God said to us, "Steve and Wendy, your hopelessness about a problem is a bigger problem than the problem." Our lack of "glistening hope" about a situation (a relationship, habit, nation, etc.) within our lives is almost always a bigger problem than the problem itself. Romans 12:2 does not say, "Be transformed by trying harder or getting a better plan." I'm all for ideas, plans, and wisdom from God, but most of the limitations and lack of breakthrough in our lives comes from believing something wrong, not doing something wrong.

We might perceive that our past is the problem. We certainly don't dismiss the fact that past traumas and pain can be a great challenge to us, but our past can't stop us (only our belief systems and conclusions about the past can). Or maybe we say our problem is the people in our lives who are limiting us. Again, we don't discount the effects of negative people, but two of my favorite Bible characters testify to us we can overcome this. David had a dad who did not believe in him, brothers who belittled him, and a king who tried to kill him; but he still fulfilled his call (1 Samuel 16:10-13; 17:28; 24:1-2). Joseph fulfilled his dream and destiny even though his brothers sold him into slavery, Potiphar's wife falsely accused him of rape, and the chief butler forgot him (Genesis 37:23-24; 39:7-23; 40:23).

The real problem in most of our "problems" is the lack of hope we have. This is something Wendy and I have learned personally, and are still growing in. I remember going to Wendy with a challenging relational situation that I was feeling hopeless about, and she said these words: "What do you need to believe to have hope about this?" This is one of the most important questions we can ask ourselves. Understanding what the real problem is will help press us into the real solution. What do you need to believe to have hope about your situation?

When we first learned about hope and joy, we thought, "Oh no, now we need to be happy too! We are trying so hard to be good Christians, and now we need to add this. It sounds like hard work!" We did not realize our lack of hope and joy was not the problem, but a symptom of a bigger problem of what we were believing. If we want a different emotion, we will need a different belief. And, the good news is that when we start believing truth, the Holy Spirit supernaturally infuses us with hope – ". . . in believing that you may abound in hope by the power of the Holy Spirit" (Romans 15:13).

Let's focus on the real problem (our lack of hope) and watch what the Lord does in and through us.

DAY 37
The Power of Our Conclusions

Our conclusions about circumstances are almost always more important than the circumstances themselves.

Today, we will examine the story of the twelve spies in Numbers 13 and 14. The spies were commissioned to give a report to Moses and the children of Israel concerning the land God had promised to them. After forty days, they came back to Moses and were divided into two groups: 1) Joshua and Caleb, and 2) the other ten spies. **Both saw the same set of circumstances but put a different conclusion to what they saw.** Again, our conclusions about circumstances are almost always more important than the circumstances themselves.

A conclusion is "an opinion or decision that is formed after a period of thought or analysis." Many factors contribute to how we make conclusions. Some of them are:

- Whether we have the habit of magnifying the Lord or magnifying the problem (Psalm 34:3)
- Whether we have been renewing our minds on spiritual faith food or worldly doubt food (Romans 12:2)
- Whether we believe God has equipped us to be victorious or not (Deuteronomy 28)
- Whether we believe that opposition to our promises is normal or not (1 Timothy 1:18)

Here are some great truths from the story of the twelve spies that will help us attach higher conclusions to the circumstances we face:

- **Future blessings motivate us to keep going and to not give in easily to fear-based conclusions** – "We went to the land where you sent us. It truly flows with milk and honey, and this is its fruit" (Numbers 13:27). Hope is the belief that the future will be better than the present, and I/we have the power to help make it so. There is something good to fight for regarding our families, cities, and nations.
- **Giants to defeat should not surprise us** – "Nevertheless the people who dwell in the land are strong; the cities are fortified and very large; moreover we saw the descendants of Anak there" (Numbers 13:28). It is in the process of overcoming these giants that we develop the character to be able to steward the promised blessings well.
- **The more we talk about our problems; the worse our conclusions get** – "The Amalekites dwell in the land of the South; the Hittites, the Jebusites, and the Amorites dwell in the mountains; and the Canaanites dwell by the sea and along the banks of the Jordan" (Numbers 13:29). As we mature, we learn to share the facts of a situation without releasing a concluding, spirit of unbelief in what we say.
- **People of courage are present in every challenge and have a different perspective** – "Then Caleb quieted the people before Moses, and said,'Let us go up at once and take possession, for we are well able to overcome it'" (Numbers 13:30). Joshua and Caleb found each other, and unlike the other 10 spies, their perspective allowed them to enter the promised land. It is wise to build relationships with people of courage now.
- **Our conclusions largely depend on what reports we listen to and receive** – "And they gave the children of Israel a bad report of the land which they had spied out, saying, 'The land through which we have gone as spies is a land that devours its inhabitants, and all the people whom we saw in it are men of great stature'" (Numbers 13:32). It takes no effort at all to be pessimistic or to have a victim mindset about the future, but we are empowered to overcome these and every obstacle we face.

- **Who we think we are will largely determine the conclusions we make about life's circumstances** – "Here we saw the giants . . .and we were like grasshoppers in our own sight, and so we were in their sight" (Numbers 13:33). It is often not what we think about God that stops us, but it is what we think about ourselves that prevents the promises from being realized.
- **Those who say they can, and those who say they can't are both right** – The ten spies said they could not win and they didn't. Joshua and Caleb said they could win and they did.

Our conclusions about the following situations are almost always more important than the situations themselves:

- Family dysfunction
- Problems at work
- National crises
- Personal weaknesses

You and I are the Joshuas and Calebs of this generation. Because we magnify the Lord, not the problem, we are increasingly concluding from faith and not fear. These hope-filled conclusions will help create a foundation for our joy to truly be our strength.

DAY 38
Delighting In Our Weakness

"But he said to me (Paul), 'My grace is sufficient for you, for my power is made perfect in weakness.' Therefore I will boast all the more gladly about my weaknesses, so that Christ's power may rest on me. That is why, for Christ's sake, I delight in weaknesses, in insults, in hardships, in persecutions, in difficulties. For when I am weak, then I am strong"

(2 Corinthians 12:9-10). NIV

The Passion Translation says verse 10 this way, "**So I will celebrate my weaknesses**, for when I'm weak I sense more deeply the mighty power of Christ living in me."

What a radical idea to celebrate our weaknesses. It sounds completely absurd, but whether our weakness is physical, emotional, relational, intellectual, or something else, we can access God's grace and strength as we do.

Here are six reasons to celebrate your weaknesses:

1. **It is an expression of faith** – As we celebrate our weaknesses, we affirm that God's perfect strength is going to show up in our lives. Faith believes before it sees, and it is better to celebrate before we see than after we see.

2. **It releases the joy of the Lord (which is our strength)** – Intentional celebration stirs up our joy. As we get excited about an area we are battling weakness in, we are going to see God's strength manifest in it.

3. **It is a practical way to delight ourselves in the Lord** – "Delight yourself in the Lord, and He will give you the desires of your heart" (Psalm 37:4). We cannot truly delight in the Lord unless we celebrate our weaknesses. If we wait to delight after we overcome all our weaknesses, we will never delight in the Lord.

4. **It is a way to magnify the Lord** – We are to magnify the Lord, not the problem (Psalm 34:3). Celebrators are continually magnifying God's love, solutions, the power of past and current prayers, and what Jesus has won on the cross for us.s

5. **It disempowers shame, guilt, and condemnation** – When our weaknesses manifest, we will be tempted to disqualify ourselves from being happy, blessed, and significant. This temptation is usually a bigger problem than anything happening through our weaknesses. However, when we choose to celebrate the weakness, then these tools of our enemy will be defeated.

6. **It causes us to focus on the supernatural (which is the solution)** – Our lack of hope is usually triggered by not factoring in and believing in the supernatural. We get discouraged because we are focused on ourselves instead of the Lord. Everytime we celebrate our weaknesses, we reaffirm the power of the Holy Spirit operating in the unseen realms of our life.

Let's join the Apostle Paul in celebrating our weaknesses. Even if we are really struggling and need counseling, intervention, medical help, or accountability concerning our struggle, it is still a secret weapon to keep the grace and strength of God flowing in our direction.

DAY 39
Never Stop Starting

I remember being a new follower of Jesus in a homegroup with our college pastor, Richard, and many other newly saved young adults. I was astounded by our born again experience. I found out as a semi-hippie that there was no high like the Most High! I was grateful that someone like Richard was always there to guide and encourage us at the beginning of our journey into Kingdom life.

Even though I had a dramatic conversion, I still struggled with some lifestyle issues and spiritual disciplines. I frequently felt like a failure. One of the things Richard taught us was this; NEVER STOP STARTING. He would say this frequently. It was a lifeline then and still is.

Here are some examples of areas to never stop starting:

- Bible reading and prayer
- Eating right
- Evangelism
- Overcoming anger
- Overcoming addictive behaviors
- Exercise
- Growing in connection with our loved ones
- Forgiving
- Doing what we love
- Learning new things

- Letting go of control and trusting God
- Walking in joy

Why we should never stop starting:

1. **Because it is part of not becoming weary in well-doing** – "And let us not grow weary while doing good, for in due season we shall reap if we do not lose heart" (Galatians 6:9).

2. **Because it teaches us to celebrate progress, not perfection** – The perfectionist mindset will not allow us to feel good about ourselves (or others) unless things are done perfectly. When we start again with hope, it is another opportunity to celebrate ourselves and overcome perfectionism.

3. **Because the only other alternative is to quit** – And when we really consider this option, it is not very appealing.

4. **Because others will benefit from it** – As we keep seeking to grow and move forward in life, we will create a breakthrough that others get to walk in. One of my favorite declarations is, "My forward movement in life causes Red Seas to part" (Exodus 14:15ff). As the sea parts, others get to walk through it too.

5. **Because we are overcomers** – We may feel like failures, but we are not failures. We are not who our past says we are, but we are who God says we are. We are "more than conquerors" (Romans 8:37) and we have already been given "a spirit of power and of love and of a sound mind" (2 Timothy 1:7).

6. **Because those who succeed most seem to fail most** – Just as a toddler learning to walk seems to be a failure in the beginning journey of walking, we too will often struggle as we seek to walk higher in different areas of life. Aren't you glad you did not stop starting in learning how to walk?

How do we never stop starting:

1. **Use wisdom learned from the past** – When I miss the mark, I do not call it failure, I call it learning. Every time I start again, I have greater wisdom in how to do things better.

2. **By involving others as needed** – We all have an area or areas where we will need to include others so we break through into consistency. As we humble ourselves and say, "I need help," it will increase the grace to do what we desire to do (James 4:6). We can involve others through accountability, having someone join us in a beneficial habit, etc.

3. **By making declarations** – "God gives life to the dead by calling those things that are not as though they are" (Romans 4:17). As we declare life ("I eat well and exercise regularly," "I am consistent in Bible reading," or "There is always a solution for every area of my life"), we strengthen the beliefs that will help us become more consistent.

4. **By making more achievable goals** – If writing is a struggle in this season, it's better to write two minutes a day than nothing, even if the "ideal" goal is to write 10 hours a week. If you're struggling to exercise every day, try exercising twice a week. Twice a week with celebration is better than no times a week with an accusing, perfectionist mindset.

5. **By understanding everyone has to start again** – One of the biggest lies we are tempted to believe is that we are the only ones who struggles to develop consistency in important areas of life. No, we are all making adjustments that require us to start again on a regular basis.

6. **By delighting in the Lord** – "Delight yourself also in the Lord, and He shall give you the desires of your heart" (Psalm 37:4). As we say, "Lord, I cannot wait to see how you are going to help me be consistent in this area!", we activate the strength of the joy of the Lord (Nehemiah 8:10).

"Never stop starting." These words changed my life years ago and still do. Let's never stop starting in rejoicing in the Lord, delighting in Him, having a merry heart, creating a culture of gladness around us, enjoying life, and being a cheerful decider.

DAY 40
Reflection, Activation, and Advanced Research on Joy

Advanced Research on Joy by Dr. Pieter Lagaay
Joy and Marriage

Having joy in any relationship, whether it is with a spouse, children, or family, is a part of how humanity would categorize a relationship as being successful. The expression "A happy wife is a happy life" as it pertains to marriage is only half true and commonly misunderstood. A 2007 meta-analysis of 93 studies found that marriage quality depended most on individual joy in both spouses. The models used in most of these studies to ascertain the quality of a marriage are the "stress generation model" and the "marital discord model of depression."

In 2013, a study aimed to predict joy in a marriage based on the two quality of marriage models mentioned above. The study found that individually joyful spouses who make decisions together successfully predicted a higher marriage quality. This study inferred that empowering your spouse increases the likelihood of having a higher-quality marriage. The prediction model of this study found that empowering joy is key to a successful relationship, whether it is with your spouse, child, or family member.

Although several studies have demonstrated the causal relationship between individual joy and marriage quality, newer studies have found joy is imparted onto another person through joyful empowerment. A 2015 study in the journal of Human Brain Mapping tested whether expressed (verbal) or implied (nonverbal) joy through empowerment from a spouse would elicit a neurobehavioral response of joy in the other spouse. What was fascinating regarding the results of the fMRI scans was that greater neural processing was found from implied cues of joy and empowerment than from expressed cues. The study concluded that people in a deeply committed relationship who perceive joy and empowerment from the other person are more likely to feel joy themselves.

Before Jesus conveyed His commandment to love one another to His disciples and empowered them with what was to come at the last supper, He reminded them, "These things I have spoken to you, that My joy may remain in you, and that your joy may be full." (John 15:11). (This verse is a good one to meditate on.) As Christians, we are to be full of joy as we love others. The empowering covenant made with Jesus is in love and full of joy. The covenant of marriage, parenting, or family is no different. This scripture supports the studies mentioned above. Joy in a person strengthens the quality of a deeply committed relationship; if a person lacks joy, it can be imparted through empowering love.

Note: Even though this devotional targets married couples, you can apply these principles and this activation to important relationships in your life.

Activation

- Plan 20 minutes with your spouse or someone you want to connect with. Each person gets 10 minutes to speak.
- During this time, only the person who has the time is permitted to speak but is not required to.
- Whatever the person with the time does, the purpose is to make the other person feel loved and perceive the joy that is in their heart.
- The person with the time should aim to empower the other through encouragement and unconditional love.

- After 10 minutes, switch.
- When both people have each had a turn, tell the other person if you feel more joyful and what was said or done that impacted you the most.

Congratulations! You have completed your 40 Days of Joy! Here are some ideas for how to keep growing in joy:

- Do this 40 day journey with someone else or a group of people.
- Read more of Steve's books on joy and laughter.
- Enroll in Igniting Hope Academy online courses to increase your hope and joy.

APPENDIX

FULLY CONVINCED: THE ART OF DECISION MAKING

Attaching faith to what we do and who we are is one of the most important things we can do for effective living. Doubt cripples our joy, our influence, and our connection with God. This is a powerful book that will help you develop a healthy process in decision-making, increase your energy and joy and unlock the incredible gifts that are in you. Abad decision made in faith has a greater likelihood of success than a good decision made in doubt. "One person esteems one day above another; another esteems every day alike. Let each be fully convinced in his own mind." (Romans 14:5)

DECLARE IT: INCLUDES DECLARATIONS FOR 96 DIFFERENT LIFE SITUATIONS

If we are going to experience something higher, we need to believe something higher. If we are going to believe something higher, we need to hear something higher than what we are feeling and experiencing. Declarations are faith statements about what is true but is not fully yet in our experience. One of the greatest ways to activate our faith and renew our minds is to declare truth. This book provides powerful, biblically-based truths to declare for almost every conceivable situation we will face in life.

IGNITING HOPE IN 40 DAYS

This book will truly ignite your hope. We believe you will become convinced that hope is the belief that the future will be better than the present, and you have the power to help make it so Our hope level determines our influence level. Our hopelessness about a problem is a bigger problem than the problem. And so much more. Join Steve on a 40-Day journey to spark your faith and hope into higher levels than ever before!

THE CULTURE OF EMPOWERMENT: BUSINESS AND ORGANIZATION EDITION

Have you ever been championed by someone – a person who believed in you more than you believe in yourself, and who told you, "YOU CAN DO IT!"? Their belief in you became a rock to stand on against the waves of insecurity, doubt, and fear in your mind. They were willing to allow you to try something challenging and new under their mentorship, and it caused you to find out there was more in you than you thought.

IGNITING FAITH IN 40 DAYS

There must be special seasons in our lives when we break out of routine and do something that will ignite our faith about God and our identity in Christ. This book will lead you through the life-changing experience of a 40-day negativity fast. This fast teaches the power of declaring truth and other transforming daily customs that will strengthen your foundation of faith and radically increase your personal hope.

VICTORIOUS MINDSETS

What we believe is ultimately more important than what we do. The course of our lives is set by our deepest core beliefs (mindsets).
These mindsets are either a stronghold for God's purposes or a playhouse for the enemy of our souls. Steve Backlund reveals 50 biblical attitudes that are foundational for those who desire to walk in freedom and power, including lies to overcome, declarations to strengthen each mindset, and practical wisdom.

THE CULTURE OF EMPOWERMENT

Have you ever been championed by someone? Their belief in you became a rock to stand on against the waves of insecurity, doubt, and fear in your mind. This book reveals a solid biblical foundation for living a lifestyle of empowerment. Through empowering people, Jesus set an example for us and revealed the Father's heart in doing so. The Culture of Empowerment gives insight and practical tools for championing people as well as developing empowering beliefs about yourself and others.

LIVING FROM THE UNSEEN

Living from the unseen realm reveals that we can live life through the eyes of the spirit and with an awareness of the spiritual realities and principles that affect our everyday lives. This is a book that shares insights on how to obtain a transformed life through renewing the mind. Wendy's journey, and these insights, are meant for those Christians who intuitively know there is more to "walking in the Spirit" than traditionally understood by the Church. This book will help identify beliefs that block the reception of God's blessings and hinder our ability to live out our destiny.

LET'S JUST LAUGH AT THAT FOR KIDS: 1&2

We all want the best for the young people in our lives. This book will help you set children up for success by teaching them to replace lies with truth and to take a combative stance against beliefs that try to hold them back. This book is an interactive journey in taking every thought captive with the kids you love. Through these fun, laughter–filled pages, we expose twenty common lies kids often believe, and this book helps train them to use "laughter weapons" to disarm the lies. We then use Scripture, declarations, and practical wisdom to reinforce the truth.

LET'S JUST LAUGH AT THAT

Our hope level is an indicator of whether we are believing truth or lies. Truth creates hope and freedom, but believing lies brings hopelessness and restriction. We can have great theology but still be powerless because of deception about the key issues of life.

Many of these self-defeating mindsets exist in our subconscious and have never been identified. This book will expose numerous falsehoods and reveal the truth that will make us free. Get ready for a joy-infused adventure into hope-filled and impactful living.

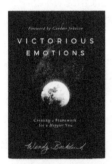

VICTORIOUS EMOTIONS

This book is about renovating and reconstructing the pathways and strongholds of our thinking. It explores how our brains create certain belief systems and how to intentionally create new ones. The goal of this book is not to focus on eliminating negative emotions, but to build a tidal wave of victorious emotions that are pulled into our lives as easily and surely as the ocean tides will appear every day. It is time to be overtaken by emotions that lead us into victory!

YOU'RE CRAZY IF YOU DON'T TALK TO YOURSELF

Jesus did not just think His way out of the wilderness and neither can we. He spoke truth to invisible beings and mindsets that sought to restrict and defeat Him. This book reveals that life and death are truly in the power of the tongue, and emphasize the necessity of speaking truth to our souls. Our words really do set the course of our lives and the lives of others (Proverbs 18:21, James 3:2-5).

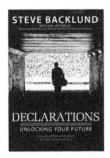

DECLARATIONS

You may be wondering "What are declarations and why are people making them?" or maybe, "Aren't declarations simply a repackaged 'name it and claim it' heresy?" This book answers these questions by sharing 30 biblical reasons for declaring truth over every area of life.The revelation this book carries will help you to set the direction your life will go. Get ready for 30 days of powerful devotions and declarations that will convince you that life is truly in the power of the tongue.

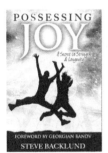

POSSESSING JOY

In His presence is fullness of joy (Psalm 16:11). Joy is to increase as we go deeper in our relationship with God. Religious tradition, however, has devalued the role that gladness and laughter have for personal victory and kingdom advancement. His presence may not always producejoy, but if we never or rarely have fullness of joy, we must reevaluate our concept of God. This book Possessing Joy will take you on a journey toward the headwaters of the full joy that Jesus often spoke of.

HELP! I'MAPASTOR

Help! I Am a Pastor addresses many common situations in church life that few seem really prepared for. It gives tools for successfully addressing these happenings with humor, healthy beliefs, and divine strategies. The truths presented by Steve Backlund will help every church leader become more proactive in his or her leadership, plus be able to equip their teams with the core values necessary to create healthy ministries. This book includes 80 life and leadership core values and 50 scenarios.

Made in the USA
Monee, IL
09 May 2023

33309315R00075